EMANCIPATION

Releasing the Power of Spiritual
Warfare in Evangelism

W. Scott Moore

Eleos Press

Rogersville, AL

Emancipation
W. Scott Moore, B.B.A, M. Div., D. Min.
© 2016

ISBN-13: 978-0692701515

Cover Design: Eleos Press, www.eleospress.com

Interior Formatting: Ellen C. Maze www.ellencmaze.com,
          The Author's Mentor

Published by Eleos Press, www.eleospress.com
Also available in eBook form

PRINTED IN THE UNITED STATES OF AMERICA

Ephesians 6:12 NIV: "For our struggle is not against flesh and blood, but against the rulers, against the authorities, against the powers of this dark world and against the spiritual forces of evil in the heavenly realms."

After reading *Emancipation,* I was reminded of the very real struggle a person called of God goes through in attempting to live for the Lord and obey His will for their life. This book reminded me just how easy it is to get sidetracked from the main purpose of witnessing and leading the lost to Christ.

As believers we face an enemy whose goal it is to defeat Christ's church. We will have to engage in this battle against this enemy until Christ's return. Reading a book like this that tells of the real struggles of real people helps us to see how the enemy has lost and the victory is the Lord's. It showed me that there will have to be sacrifices along the way, just as Christ has sacrificed for us. But it also showed me that those sacrifices are worth it when the name of one more soul is written in the Lamb's book of life because the sacrifices were made.

I encourage everyone to read this book so you can be encouraged to keep on keeping on in the fight for the lost, in the name of Jesus. There is power in no other name!!

~Bonnie McMinn, a servant of our Lord.

I have known Pastor Scott Moore since 1990 when he asked me to come to Toledo to do a two-day healing and restoration weekend for adult survivors of sexual abuse. Subsequently I relocated to Toledo and was in ministry directing a Christian counseling center there.

I have since done similar outreaches at each of his churches in Alabama. I have found him to be a true advocate for the wounded and deeply appreciate that he "keeps the MAIN thing the MAIN thing." I have been working with the broken for nearly thirty years: inner healing, deliverance, and then as a clinical pastoral counselor and Pastor Scott's book emphasizes the needed balance between evangelism, discipleship and spiritual warfare.

~Julie Christopher Weyandt MA, LPC
Founder / Director - Beauty for Ashes Counseling

Loved this book for so many reasons. Scott takes the mask off the enemy and helps us see the many different ways the enemy works in a Christian's life. Very well written and easy to read and follow, the book is hard to put down. Even when the reader thinks the enemy may have passed him by after reading this book you probably will catch yourself saying, "Ooooh, so that's what that was!" We're in a fight daily - this book is a great resource that brings the battle and what's really going on around us to a place we can identify and helps us see the resources the enemy uses as well as what we can do to fight "the good fight". Thanks Scott for sharing this with us - And you, reader! Get the book! You'll be glad you did!

~Matt McCurry

I enjoyed reading this book written by the husband of my high school friend from long ago. Scott Moore's book, *Emancipation*, is quite interesting. Written from his perspective as a Protestant minister of the Gospel, Moore continuously encourages anyone who is involved in evangelism and spiritual warfare, or in any type of ministry for that matter, to remember that "the main thing is to keep the main thing the main thing." Complete with a lot of examples from his own ministerial experiences, this book ought to be well received by anyone called to serve the Body of Christ with ministries of healing and evangelization.

~Kathryn Byrne, M.P.M.
Life Coach and Author
Understanding the Abuse of Adults by Catholic
Clergy and Religious Leaders

Dedication

This book is dedicated, first and foremost, to my Lord Jesus Christ. He is the reason for my existence and the Savior of my soul. He is the first and the last and everything in between. Thank you, Jesus, for being my best friend and elder brother in this life and the next!

This book is also dedicated to my wife, Diane. She has stood by me faithfully for nearly forty years. She is my most prized and cherished "possession." She is the one person, this side of heaven that knows me the best and still loves me the most.

I would also like to mention several of my spiritual mentors:

- In the area of evangelism my mentors have been Leonard Hampton, Dr. Gray Allison, and Jackie Shelton. Additionally, "Brother Jackie" was the first man to hire me after I graduated from the seminary. He and I shared a wonderful ministry together as we led scores of people to faith in Jesus Christ.

- My mentors in the area of missions have been Dr. Gray Allison, Dr. Steve Wilkes, and Jaime Boyachek.

- In the area of spiritual warfare, I want to thank the man that helped me to further understand spiritual battles and how to win them— evangelist Leandro "Lee" Castro.

- In the area of prayer, my thanks go to Harold Meaux, a saint now in Heaven with the Lord Jesus Christ. He welcomed me into his church each morning as a group of us shared some of the best corporate prayer meetings we have ever experienced.

Table of Contents

Preface

I have experienced, by the grace of God, success in both the areas of evangelism and spiritual warfare. Over the years I have observed that, by far, most Christians are much more interested in hearing the warfare stories than they are in hearing the evangelism stories. And, I must admit, they *are* exciting.

A popular nursery rhyme posited the question: "Is your porridge too hot, too cold or just right?" In keeping with that theme, what is the proper balance between evangelism and spiritual warfare?

The Bible teaches that Christians are in a constant battle with an unseen enemy. The Apostle Paul wrote in Ephesians 6:10-12:

> *Finally, be strong in the Lord and in the strength of His might. Put on the full armor of God, so that you will be able to stand firm against the schemes of the devil. For our struggle is not against flesh and blood, but against the rulers, against the powers, against the world forces of this darkness, against the spiritual forces of wickedness in the heavenly places.*

The Bible also teaches that we are to be His witnesses throughout the earth.[1] A favorite saying of the evangelist Ron Dunn was, "the main thing is to keep the main thing the main thing."[2] He was, of course, referring to evangelism: leading people to a saving knowledge of Jesus Christ as their personal Lord and Savior. The one thing that is better than having success in spiritual warfare is having success in one's evangelistic endeavors.

---

[1] Acts 1:8.

[2] http://www.rondunn.com/Biography.htm, website visited on 9/24/2011.

My desire is that you, my dear reader, will keep that thought in mind as you read this book. Keep on keeping the main thing the main thing.

~ Scott Moore, November 25, 2011

NOTE: Accounts in Phases One: Evangelism and Phase Two: Evangelistic Confrontation will overlap chronologically. Both sections contain accounts of my seminary experiences and my service as a youth minister at Pleasant Grove Baptist Church.

Evangelism

Long before I was involved in spiritual warfare, I became committed to the main thing: lifestyle evangelism.

The Start

The Precipitating Factor

My dad died at the age of 52. I was devastated! I made an appointment to speak with our pastor, Bill Ricketts. I offered to do maintenance work around the church. The pastor wisely responded, "We have a maintenance staff here at the church. But I would like to invite you to do something else." I asked, "What is it, Brother Bill?" He said, "Come to visitation on Tuesday nights. You won't have to say anything; you

4

will become a 'prayer partner;' your only job will be to pray for your 'witnessing partner' as he shares his faith with lost people." Reluctantly, I agreed.

Leonard Hampton

I arrived at the church at the appointed time on the following Tuesday night for visitation. I was assigned to work with my first, and only, visiting partner. His name was Leonard Hampton; he held a PhD in forestry, and was employed by the University of Georgia.-

L-R: Leonard Hampton and Scott at Scott's ordination service.

Leonard was, first and foremost, a soul-winner. He loved to win people to faith in Jesus Christ. He told me on one occasion that whenever a new employee would begin working in his department at the university that he would tell him or her about Jesus.

Leonard would arrive at the church on Tuesday nights and the pastor would ask, "Leonard, did you win anybody to Christ this week?" Leonard would usually say something like, "Yes Brother Bill. I saw three people trust Christ this week. But may I tell you about one." And then he would proceed to tell his story to the rest of us in the room.

I not only had the privilege of hearing about his exploits, but I also had the privilege of watching him in action. He would begin with small talk, but would move quickly to the purpose of our visit: to share Christ with our prospects. I don't remember anyone accepting Jesus on his first attempt, but he would never give up. He would move a little closer, talk more softly, and patiently win people to Christ. He had a passion for reaching the unsaved!

One night after we had completed our visits, I asked Leonard a question. I said, "I have a man at work that is a Jehovah's Witness. How do I go about sharing with him?" Leonard was a man that walked with the

6

Lord; he was sensitive to the prompting of the Holy Spirit; he didn't "bite" at my question. He looked at me and said, "In order to win a Jehovah's Witness to Christ you would have to be right with God yourself. Are you as close to the Lord as you used to be?"

A good description of my response is found in Acts 2:37a: "Now when they heard this, they were pierced to the heart." I was pierced to the heart! I thought, "How did he know that?" I answered, "No, I'm not." He said, "Would you *like* to be as close to the Lord as you used to be?" I responded, "Yes, but not now. I will pray when I get home." Leonard answered, "That's fine. I will be praying for you. May I pray for you now?" I said, "Of course."

As Leonard was praying, God was speaking to me; he said, "How many times have you been convicted in church and said the same thing, 'I will take care of this as soon as I get home?'" I said in my heart, "Several times." The Holy Spirit said, "Are you going to waste another opportunity?" I thought, "No, I am not!"

7

As soon as Leonard finished praying I said, "Leonard, I have changed my mind; I want to get right with the Lord right now." He said, "That's great, Scott. Why don't you talk to the Lord in prayer and tell Him that you are coming back into a deeper relationship with Him."

I prayed, I confessed, and I wept. Leonard was ecstatic. He had seen this outcome many times before. I was repenting from my sins and returning to the Lord.

Over the months ahead, God would transform my life. Leonard was amazed at the change. He later told me, "I have never seen anyone else embrace the Christian life as you have; you are soaking it up like a sponge!"

After several months of "soaking up the Christian life like a sponge," I was sent out with Leonard and Frank Brannon as their "prayer partner." Frank Brannon was a top manager with the Life Insurance Company of Georgia.™ As far as I know, Leonard and Frank had never worked together before; they were the two most dynamic soul-winners in the church and were always training others to become witnesses for Christ. I now believe Leonard specifically requested that Frank accompany us because he was seeking a formidable conversion: a college professor at the University of Georgia.

As we drove to the professor's home I thought, "This is great. Now I will have a firsthand look at these two masters in action." I was disappointed. After the small talk, the "masters" began to share. The professor interrupted them by asking the question, "What about the heathen in Africa? Doesn't God care about them?" I looked first at Leonard and then at Frank; neither said a word. I thought, "This is easy. I can answer that question." And so I did: "There are more people committing their lives to Jesus Christ in Africa than in any other part of the world." I continued, "In fact, they are now sending missionaries from Africa to the United States."

The "masters" continued to share, but to no avail. We left the house and returned to the car. I thought, "These guys are going to praise me for being so smart." I was wrong! We drove a couple of blocks and Leonard stopped the car. He and Frank simultaneously turned around and looked at me. Leonard spoke; he said, "Scott, don't you think that Frank and I knew the answer to the professor's question?" I said, "I didn't think so. If you did, why didn't you answer?" He said, "When the devil is on the run, he will try to get you into a squirrel cage; he will motivate the person to whom you are witnessing to ask questions that will get you running around in circles. If you try to answer them, you will forget the primary purpose of your visit: to win the man to Christ." And then he gave the admonition, "Don't ever do that again!" I was hurt, but I understood his explanation: "Keep the main thing the main thing."

My First Convert

A popular story regarding Dwight L. Moody begins with his being accosted by a drunk. The man asked, "Mr. Moody, do you remember me?" Mr. Moody responded, "I'm sorry, sir, but I don't." The thick tongued man replied, "I'm one of your converts." Mr. Moody said, "You must be one of mine; you are certainly not one of God's!"

My first convert was actually God's convert *through* me. I made a solo visit to a college student named Ivan Veiken. The man was brilliant; he asked some very difficult questions. He finally hit me with his best shot, his tried and true question, "How could a loving God send anyone to Hell?"

I had no idea how to answer his question; I prayed silently. The Lord immediately gave me the answer! I glanced at his desk and spotted a quarter.[3] The quarter was on the heads' side. I pointed and asked,

---

[3] A coin worth 25 cents.

"What is this?" He smugly answered, "It's a quarter." I picked it up and flipped it over on the tails' side. I asked again, "Then what is this?" He almost laughed out loud as he said, "It's a quarter." I flipped it back to the heads' side and said, "But you told me *this* was a quarter." "It is," he replied. At the risk of being absurd, I flipped it one more time as I asked, "Then how can this be a quarter?" He replied, "They are just two sides of the same coin."

In tennis lingo, I had "point, set, and match." I asked, "If a quarter can have two sides, could it be possible that God would also has two sides? Couldn't He be both a God of love *and* a God of judgment?" I watched in wonder as the man's eyes and face literally lit up. He said, "I guess He could." In a matter of moments, he prayed to receive Jesus Christ as his Lord and Savior.

The Surge

Seminary

Although I continued to share my faith with many people, Ivan was the one and only person to come to Christ through my personal witness. My evangelistic prowess, however, was about to change. God led me to attend the Mid-America Baptist Theological Seminary in Memphis, Tennessee.[4] The seminary trustees had established one major requirement for course credit: every student needed to witness to one unsaved person every week while enrolled in classes. And, as I would soon discover, that included *me*.

The witnessing requirement, unchanged to this day, is as follows:[5]

---

[4] Mid-America is now located in Cordova, Tennessee.
[5] Mid-America Baptist Theological Seminary 2011 Catalog, pg. 61.

All enrolled students must witness to an average of at least one person per week during the semester. To constitute a personal witness, the interview is to include a presentation of the plan of salvation to a person believed to be unsaved and an invitation for that person to receive Jesus Christ as Lord and Savior. The essential elements of the Gospel—faith in Jesus Christ alone and repentance of sin—are what the Seminary holds to be necessary for salvation. In order to fulfill the personal witnessing requirement, no other element should be involved in the Gospel witness (i.e., baptism, church membership, etc.)

Dr. Gray Allison

Dr. B. Gray Allison, known affectionately as "Dr. Gray," was, and is, the greatest soul-winner I have ever met. Dr. Gray was the seminary's counterpart to Leonard Hampton. Now in his eighties, Dr. Gray's primary focus in life has been to take as many people with him to Heaven as he possibly can.

What has motivated Dr. Gray to consistently share his faith throughout the years? He told us a story in Evangelism class one day of how God kept leading him to approach a childhood friend to tell him about Jesus Christ. Dr. Gray had good intentions, but he kept putting it off. One day his friend was killed in an automobile accident; Dr. Gray was devastated. He thought, "My friend is in Hell right now because I wouldn't take the time to tell him about the Lord." He then told us, "Men, any time I begin to lose my evangelistic zeal I get in my car and drive to the cemetery in Louisiana. I look at my friend's tombstone and ask God to forgive me." He then said, "It doesn't take long for the motivation to return."

A typical sharing time on Tuesday mornings included this statement from Dr. Gray: "I have had the privilege of leading several people to Christ this week." And then he would challenge the student body with this: "I am not talking about the people that received Christ as a result of my sermons during the revival last week; many were saved during that time as well. I am talking about face-to-face time spent in people's homes sharing Christ with them." He would then make his point: "I know you men are busy with class work, and many of you have jobs. But I am a seminary president, a teacher, and a full-time evangelist. I spend a lot of time traveling from one place to another. If *I* can find the time to witness, you can, too."

I found myself somewhat deficient in my witnessing endeavors after the first few weeks of my first semester; I would have to make up for lost time in order to receive credit for my class work. I made an appointment to see "Dr. Gray." He welcomed me into his office. I said, "Dr. Gray, I am delinquent in meeting my witnessing requirements." He asked, "How far behind are you?" I said, "I haven't witnessed to anyone." He replied, "You can make it up; just share Christ with six people next week." I said, "That might be a little hard. I am really busy with my class work." He said, "That's okay. Don't worry about it." I asked, "Really? It's okay?" He said, "Yes, we offer the same classes again next year. You can make them over again then." I looked askance. I said, "You're serious, aren't you?" He replied, "I am *very* serious!" And I could tell that he was.

I became serious; I asked, "How can I possibly find six people to witness to in one week?" Dr. Gray said, "Why don't you go to the Laundromat around the corner? You could witness to the people as they come in to wash their clothes." I followed his advice and, in a couple of hours, witnessed to six people about their need to accept Christ.

I eventually enjoyed witnessing or, rather, was consumed by it. A classmate announced to everyone in chapel one Tuesday morning, "I have found it!" We all looked curiously at him as he continued, "I have found the best spiritual fishing spot in all of Memphis, Tennessee!" He definitely had our attention. And then he told us, "It's in the low-income public housing project. The people there are extremely open to the Gospel." He then proceeded to invite those of us that might be interested in hearing more of the details to meet with him after the service. I was the first in line. Actually, I was the *only* one in line.

My classmate and I made an appointment to meet together and walk to the housing project. The day finally came and we started on our journey. Along the way, he stopped two or three people and witnessed to them. I believe one of them prayed to receive Christ. We arrived at our destination and he continued to share his faith; others prayed as well. I was hooked.

A few weeks later my classmate transferred to another seminary. I had a choice to make: I could either stop going, or take up where he left off. Thankfully, I chose the latter. Every week I would go to the housing project; every week I would see one or more precious souls won to faith in Jesus Christ.

I was never worried about my safety, although several people warned me of the dangers associated with the housing project. On one occasion I heard gunshots, and watched as a man ran out of an apartment holding his hand over a bullet wound to his forehead; he drove himself to the hospital.

On another occasion, I was speaking to three men. After introducing myself as a Bible student, one of them accused me of being a policeman. I showed him my Bible and asked, "Would a policeman be carrying one of these?" He replied, "Maybe he would, but if you were really a Bible student you would give us a ride home." I replied, "Let's go. Walk with me to my car and I will give you a ride."

On the way back, the seminary vice-president, Dr. Phil Allison, saw the four of us walking together. He later told me, "I didn't know whether to pray for *you* or for *them*!" I am thrilled to report that, by the time we reached their house, all three of them had prayed to receive Jesus Christ as their Lord and Savior!

On several other occasions, I remember walking past strangers on the street and wondering, "Is that person saved?" I would actually turn around, stop them, and engage them in a conversation in order to ask the all-important question: "Would you like to receive Jesus Christ as your personal Lord and Savior?" At the peak of my seminary career, I was personally seeing an average of three people praying the sinner's prayer each week.

My approach was simple. I would say, "Hello, my name is Scott Moore. Do you have a minute to talk?" Most people would say, "Yes," and I would proceed. "I am studying to be a preacher at that Bible school over there." And then I would point to the seminary.

My formula worked well until, one day, a man suggested I refrain from telling people that I was studying to be a preacher. He said, "In *this* community, a preacher is someone that drives a big car, makes a lot of money, and has the phone numbers of all of the women in the church. Just tell people you are studying the Bible." So I changed my script to reflect his advice.

My new and improved approach became, "Hello, my name is Scott Moore. Do you have a minute to talk? I am a student, and I attend that Bible school over there. Could I share a few Bible verses with you?" Again, most people would say, "Yes." I would then give them my modified version of the Romans' Road plan of salvation. Even though I had memorized the verses, I would follow Dr. Gray's advice to turn in my pocket New Testament to the various verses as I explained their meanings.

"Romans 3:23 says, 'For all have sinned and come short of the glory of God.' That means that all of us, at one time or another, have disobeyed God. We disobey God every time we tell a lie, or when we disobey the authorities in our lives. Have you ever disobeyed God?" Again, they would usually answer, "Yes."

"Romans 6:23 says, 'For the wages of sin is death.' A wage is like a paycheck. It is something we deserve. Let's say you go to work for a week, and your boss says, 'Listen, I can't pay you this week; if you will keep working, next week I will pay you for two weeks' work.'" I would then ask, "How long would you work for this man before you finally realized he wasn't going to pay you?" They would say, "Not long."

I would then respond, "God pays His bills. He says in His Word that you deserve death, and He will give it to you. The bad news is there are two kinds of death. The first kind of death occurs when you and I leave this world. The second kind is eternal separation from God. Romans 6:23 is saying that, because of your sin, you and I deserve to be eternally separated from God." I would close my Bible and say, "Well, that's it. Have a great day." I would smile and ask, "That's not very good news, is it?"

I would continue with the second part of the verse. It says, "But the gift of God is eternal life through Jesus Christ our Lord." I would tell them, "A gift is different from a wage. A wage is something I earn; it is something I deserve. A gift is something that someone else has earned and he or she deserves, but they have chosen to give to me. Someone else has paid for your eternal life; His name is Jesus Christ. It cost God everything when Jesus died on the cross, but it will cost you nothing. Isn't that good news?"

They would agree and I would continue. "Romans 5:8 says, 'But God commendeth[6] his love toward us, in that, while we were yet sinners, Christ died for us.' That means that, even while you were walking away from God in sin and while you were His enemy, He loved you enough to die for you. That's real love, isn't it?"

Next I would turn to Romans 10:13. "This verse says, 'For whosoever shall call upon the name shall be

---

[6] Or "shows."

saved.' That means you! If you will call upon His name He give you will eternal life as a gift. God wants to see two things in your life when He gives you that gift. Acts 20:23 says, 'repentance toward God and faith toward our Lord Jesus Christ.' Repentance simply means to turn around. You have been walking away from God through sin. Are you willing to turn around and live your life His way?"

"'And faith toward our Lord Jesus Christ' means you believe that He died on the cross to pay for your sins, and that you are willing to make Him the *Lord* of your life; you are willing to let Him become the *boss* of your life. Will you trust in Him and surrender your will in service for Him?"

If they agreed, I would lead them through the sinner's prayer with one important caveat: "The prayer I am about to pray is the prayer that *I* would pray if I wanted to accept Jesus. The words are not magical. I want this prayer to be *your* prayer. So listen carefully. If you don't understand what I am saying, or you

24

disagree, tell me to stop." And then I would always relate this story:

> *I was leading a man through a similar prayer. When I said, "Dear God, I know that I am a sinner," he said, "Stop!" I asked, "Why?" He said, "I'm not a sinner." I explained that a sinner is simply someone that has disobeyed God at some point in their lives. He said, "Then I am a sinner." I asked if he was ready to continue. He said, "Yes." I proceeded, "Dear God; he said, 'Dear God.' I know that I am a sinner; he repeated, 'I know that I am a sinner.'"*

I continued with the current witness, "So if at any time in the prayer you have a question, just stop me."[7] My typical sinner's prayer: "Dear God, I know that I am a sinner. I know that, from time to time, I have disobeyed You. I know that, because of my sin, I don't deserve to go to Heaven. But I believe that

---

[7] For the record: no one else has ever stopped me again for clarification.

Jesus died for me; that He paid for my sins on the cross. Right now, Lord Jesus, I turn away from my sins and I turn back to You. Come into my life, Lord Jesus, and save me. In Jesus' name I pray, Amen."

First Ministerial Assignment

After my graduation from the seminary in 1984, the Lord opened a wonderful door of service for me as the minister of youth at the Pleasant Grove Baptist Church in Moulton, Alabama. I didn't know much about working with teenagers but, by the grace of God, I learned quickly!

Jackie Shelton

Jackie Shelton, the pastor of Pleasant Grove, and I shared a passion for reaching the unsaved with the Gospel of Jesus Christ. He told me, "I am going to keep doing what I am already doing. You need to ask the Lord what He wants you to do, and do it."

Jackie kept his promise to keep doing what he was doing. He was undoubtedly the hardest working pastor I had ever seen. He would get up at 4:00 in the morning to pray; he

L-R: Jackie Shelton and wife, Ben-Ann

wouldn't stop working until 11:00 at night. Jackie would visit in several hospitals around the state almost every day. He personally visited in 50 homes a week. He gave half of his income back to the church. And he witnessed for Christ: he had a passion for souls! He truly was a man on a mission.

A rather humorous aside occurred one Monday morning at a Pastors' Conference. John Crawford, an older retired pastor, stated, "I got up this morning at 3:30. As I was praying, God said…" The rest of us turned to look at Jackie. You could see his mind beginning to work. He was thinking, "This guy is getting up earlier than I am."

After the Conference dismissed, John said, "Do you think I ought to tell Jackie the real reason I got out of bed at 3:30? I am an old man; my *body* wakes me." One of the other pastors said, "Don't tell him." And he didn't.

The next Monday morning Jackie said, "This morning at *3:00* as I was praying, God said…" I thought, "What a cruel joke they had played on him!"

Jackie had been a successful businessman buying cotton futures in the commodities' market, but he had an intense desire to reach people from the lower class. We started two bus routes that eventually expanded to six. We were picking up 70 or more children for church each Sunday.

Some of the other pastors in the area began to complain: "Your church bus drives right past my church every Sunday." Jackie simply replied, "If you want these barefooted bus children in your church, just tell me. I will instruct our van driver to drop them on your front doorstep." No one ever accepted his offer.

Another pastor jokingly said to me, "I heard you called Jackie from Birmingham last Sunday." Birmingham is almost 100 miles from Moulton. I asked, "What are you talking about?" He answered, "You called to tell him that one of the buses had broken down." I laughingly responded, "We don't go *that* far."

And so it has always been; envious pastors tend to make fun of the effective ones.

With all of his successes, Jackie refused to boast about his accomplishments. On one occasion, we had 60 people saved in a four-day revival. Someone said, "Hey, Jackie, I hear great things are happening at Pleasant Grove!" He replied, "God is good."

I asked him, "Why don't you share what God is doing?" He said, "I have been on the receiving end of pompous pastors and their empty boasting before; the rest of us listened to their exploits and we were discouraged. I vowed that, if God ever blessed my ministry, I would never do that to anyone else." And he was true to his word.

Jackie and I informally challenged each other to win souls for Jesus Christ. Proverbs 27:17 was certainly true of our relationship: "iron sharpens iron, so one man sharpens another." In three years we saw more than 250 people come to faith in Jesus Christ and follow Him in believers' baptism!

Phase Two:
Evangelistic Confrontation

We had a saying at the insurance company where I used to be employed: "It worked so well I quit doing it." The concept basically means that we all share a tendency to stop doing the activities that have made us successful in order to try new activities that will probably fail.

The early disciples were no exception. Jesus commissioned them to go before Him to various cities to prepare the way for His arrival. Their main assignment was to do "the main thing"—tell the inhabitants about the coming Savior. But something else happened. The early disciples had their first taste of success in spiritual warfare, and they were excited!

They said, in Luke 10:17, "Lord, even the demons are subject to us in Your name." "That's great," Jesus might have said, and then He replied in Luke 10:18-20:

I was watching Satan fall from heaven like lightning. Behold, I have given you authority to tread on serpents and scorpions, and over all the power of the enemy, and nothing will injure you. Nevertheless do not rejoice in this, that the spirits are subject to you, but rejoice that your names are recorded in heaven

I have given a great deal of consideration to Jesus' response to His disciples. At one point I thought He was telling them that sometimes the old tricks just don't seem to work; you can bind Satan and he still seems to win the victory! And there is some merit to that idea.

But, as I will need to learn and relearn many times throughout my ministry, "the main thing is to keep the main thing the main thing." Having one's name written in the Lamb's book of life is *infinitely* better than having power over the enemy.[8] Even Judas Iscariot apparently had some success in spiritual warfare as he went out with a partner in Luke's account.[9] And yet he obviously lacked the most important thing—a personal, saving relationship with the Messiah. Helping other people have their names written in the book of life through salvation, the "main thing," is a better investment of your time than enjoying the momentary excitement of a spiritual conquest.

And yet, like the early disciples, I also gradually lost my focus on "the main thing" when I began to be fascinated by spiritual warfare. I was, at first, frightened by the horror stories others were telling about their experiences in warfare. Coupled with the horror stories, however, were stories of successful encounters told by several trusted sources. Finally, I

---

[8] Revelation 21:27.
[9] Luke 10:1.

personally began to dabble in spiritual warfare and gradually became intrigued by the amazing power that God exercises over Satan and the forces of Hell.

The Start

I was young and impressionable when I entered the seminary. My fellow seminarians and I heard horror stories in the classroom about spiritual warfare. We were given the following reasons as to why we should not get involved:

- "You should avoid warfare unless you are completely prayed up and all your sins are confessed!"
- "Several men were casting a demon out of a man. The demoniac began naming all of the secret sins of each man in the group."
- "Spiritual warfare is only for the spiritually mature—new Christians need to avoid it at all

costs."

- "Satan is much too powerful; leave *him* alone and he will leave *you* alone."

And the list goes on.

Like many of my contemporaries, I took these admonitions to heart. And there *appears* to be some Biblical basis for these warnings. The city of Ephesus was known as a haven for witchcraft. The seven sons of the Jewish priest, Sceva, were less than successful in their attempt to cast out demons. In fact, they barely managed to escape with their lives.[10] The good news is, however, that the success of Paul and the failure of the seven sons of Sceva were not based upon a possession of personal power, but rather upon whether or not they had a relationship with the Lord Jesus Christ.[11]

Many of the horror stories we hear today that warn of the dangers of dealing with spiritual darkness are

---

[10] Acts 19:11-20.
[11] Acts 19:15.

simply a fabrication of the Enemy to keep God's people from taking away from him what he believes to be his rightful territory and his followers. Satan's primary objective is to keep people from knowing the truth, and thereby setting the captives free.

Someone has said, "The devil fears the weakest Christian on his or her knees." And that, my dear reader, is absolutely true.

Warfare Accounts from Others

I have heard some great stories in my time. The first story I can remember came from an evangelist named Mike Gilchrist. He told about a revival service he once held in which a man walked down the aisle of the church in the middle of his sermon. The man said, "I have a word from God!" Mike replied, "I have the pulpit; sit down!"

The man repeated, "I have a word from God!" Mike said again, "I have the pulpit; sit down!" The man said a third time, "I have a word from God." Mike

36

said, "I command you, in the name of Jesus, to sit down and be quiet." The man acted as he had been instructed; he sat on the front pew and never uttered another word.

Mike said that he finished the message, spoke with attendees at the back door, and was heading to his car when a man came running after him. "Brother Mike," he shouted, "I need you to come with me!" Mike replied, "What's the problem?" The man continued, "That man—the one you told to sit down and be quiet—he can't get up! Will you please come and release him?" Needless to say, I was impressed with Mike Gilchrist!

I heard a second story while attending an Institute in Basic Life Principles™ seminar led by Bill Gothard. He was talking about a young Marine that had attended one of his previous conferences. The man approached Bill during one of the breaks to tell him about some unusual occurrences that were taking place in his life.

Bill asked a small group of men to meet with the two of them in a smaller room. Bill talked to the man about the blood of Jesus Christ. The man immediately manifested several characteristics of demonic possession: he fell on the floor, began to writhe around, and spoke in a voice that could only be described as "otherworldly." Bill asked, "What right do you have to control this man?" The demon replied, "He has books." Bill asked, "What kinds of books?" The voice said, "Magic books, books with incantations, and sorcery."

Bill commanded the demon to leave the man. The man returned to his right mind. Bill told him about Jesus Christ and how he could have eternal life. The man prayed to receive Christ and was fully delivered. Bill advised the man to go home and burn the books.[12] The man promised that he would.

---

[12] Acts 19:18-20.

Bill then challenged those of us in attendance to also go home and pray about items in our homes that we needed to remove: rock music, pictures with small demonic icons embedded, etc. My wife and I didn't know about anyone else, but we certainly followed his counsel!

First Encounter

I was required to take a Christian counseling class in the seminary. The professor was a licensed psychiatrist. We all thought the seminary president had hired him because so many of us students were losing our minds!

We had heard rumors of one of the professor's personal experiences with spiritual warfare. And then, one day, he told our class, "I used to believe that demons did not exist. I was a member of the group that claimed that the only reason Jesus spoke of demonic possession was so that He could relate to the people of His day in terms that they could comprehend. Jesus knew that the so-called

39

'demoniacs' were really either experiencing psychological problems or had some kind of chemical imbalance. But, since His contemporaries did not have the books and the knowledge we have today, He simply healed them using the terminology of His day. Someone challenged me to participate in an exorcism at one of the larger churches in the area. I was open to this invitation, but maintained my air of professional skepticism."

The professor continued, "The minister ushered a young lady into his office. She began to act in a very unusual manner. She became wild-eyed; she spoke in indistinguishable guttural tones. The minister commanded her to remain in her chair. She obeyed, but began to slide the chair around the room. I was horrified! The minister continued to work with her using a technique with which I was unfamiliar. When he finished, the woman was sitting in his office 'in her right mind!'[13] The woman left the office. The

---

[13] Luke 8:35.

minster looked at me as he said, 'Now do you believe?' I replied, 'Yes, I do!'"

A few weeks after hearing the professor's story, my daughter began to experience night terrors. She would scream loudly in her sleep without waking up. I approached the professor after class the next day and asked, "What do you think might be causing this?" He replied, "It *could* be Satan!" I protested, "But she is only a child! What could she have possibly done for this to have happened?" He returned, "She hasn't done anything. But it is possibly the result of some occult background in her ancestry—either from one of your family members or one of your wife's family members."

I was skeptical, but I wanted to help my daughter. I asked, "What should I do?" He replied, "The next time it happens, you need to go into her room and command Satan to leave her alone." I asked, "But what authority do *I* have to tell Satan to do anything?" He answered, "You are a believer in Jesus Christ.

You belong to Him. His blood is covering you and your sins. You have the victory in Jesus."

The professor then recommended a book entitled, *Demons in the World Today: A Study of Occultism in the Light of God's Word* by Merrill F. Unger. I bought it and read it. My wife warned me to stop: "Please don't bring that book into our house! I am afraid that Satan will attack our children!" Thankfully, I didn't listen to her protestations!

A few nights later, my wife and two children were all asleep; I was still awake studying in preparation for a test at the seminary the next morning. My daughter screamed out! I ran in and began to pray, "Dear Jesus, please bind Satan from her!"

Flashback time: I thought, "But what about all the warnings and disclaimers? Is Satan going to point out all of my sins and shortcomings?" But, again, I wanted to help my daughter. I continued, "Please set her free from this!" And the Lord did! And, for the record, Satan *didn't* point out all of my sins!

Failure

My first experience with a bona fide demoniac occurred at the gas station where I worked during my last two years in the seminary. We had an alcoholic that regularly staggered into our restroom to pass out and sleep through the night. The only name anyone knew him by was "Ace."

One day, "Ace" came to the station and he looked great! He had shaved, gotten a haircut, and looked like a different man! We all told him how much better he looked. He replied, "My friend 'Big Man' died last night; I decided to straighten out my life."

A month later he returned to the gas station. He looked worse than we had ever seen him. My mind raced to the passage in Matthew 12:43-45:

Now when the unclean spirit goes out of a man, it passes through waterless places seeking rest, and does not find it. Then it says, "I will return to my house from which I came"; and when it comes, it finds it unoccupied, swept, and put in order. Then it goes and takes along with it seven other spirits more wicked than itself, and they go in and live there; and the last state of that man becomes worse than the first. That is the way it will also be with this evil generation.

"Ace" began to point at a car in the back of the parking lot. He, like the woman in Dr. Davidson's story, became wild-eyed; he laughed. I asked, "What are you laughing at, Ace?" He replied as he pointed, "That car—the wheels are turning but it is standing still!"[14]

And then he erupted in an otherworldly cacophony. I looked at the other gas station attendant—another

---

[14] Note: this was years *before* they invented the hubcaps that turn while the car is stationary!

seminary student. I asked, "What do you know about casting out demons?" He replied, "Nothing!" I said, "Let's get out of here!" Like the seven sons of Sceva, we both ran into the office and locked the door.

First Successes

My initial success in spiritual warfare occurred toward end of my three-year tenure as youth minister at Pleasant Grove Baptist Church. I saw two major victories: the liberation of an unsaved man and the deliverance of a Christian.

The Liberation of an Unsaved Man

A friend of mine, John Montgomery, and I led a prayer meeting five days a week at the local high school. One morning, one of my teens asked me to visit with a young man named "Stephan." "Brother Scott," she said, "he doesn't believe in *anything*! Will you please go and talk to him?"

I agreed. I took one of the teenage boys from our church's youth group with me to make the visit. My visiting partner stayed with Stephan's brother as Stephan and I talked; we began to walk along a trail behind his house. I asked him, "Is it true that you don't believe in God?" He replied, "There are no God, no devil, no Heaven, and no Hell. And that book you hold in your hand, the Bible, is simply a book that has been written by men; there is nothing special about it."

I asked him, "What *do* you believe in, Stephan?" He replied "The old Indian ways." The light came on in my mind. After finishing Unger's book, I had read two additional books that dealt with spiritual warfare. The books, both written by Kurt E. Koch, were: *Occult ABC: Exposing Occult Practices and Ideologies* and *Occult Practices and Beliefs: A Biblical Examination from A to Z.*

I asked, "Do you practice black magic?" He answered, "No, I don't practice *black* magic."[15] Kurt Koch had written that *all* magic—*white* magic for good purposes and *black* magic for evil purposes—is from Satan. I asked, "Then do you practice *white* magic?" "Yes I do," he replied.

I said, "What I am about to do you might think I am crazy, but you will have to get in line. I am going to pray for you and then do something." I bowed my head and prayed, "Dear Jesus, please set Stephan free from Satan's grasp." I looked at Stephan and said, "Satan, in the name of Jesus and by His shed blood I command you to leave this man alone!"

Stephan was visibly shaken! I asked, "What's wrong, Stephan?" He replied, "Something just went up my spine and out!" I asked, "What is this book I am holding?" He said, "That is the Bible—the holy Word of God!" I continued, "Do you believe in Jesus?" He

---

[15] He emphasized the word "black."

quickly responded, "I believe in God, Jesus, the devil, Heaven, *and* Hell!" I asked, "Would you like to accept Jesus Christ as your Lord and Savior?" He said, "I sure would!" I led him through the sinner's prayer; he surrendered his life to Jesus Christ!

And the best news of all was that my first real encounter had truly been successful. I had combined spiritual warfare with evangelism, with the result that a young man had been saved!

The Deliverance of a Christian

The other incident occurred when John and I were praying one morning with members of our youth group that attended another high school. We would meet each morning with this group in a private home prior to going to the aforementioned high school each morning.

Rickey, an elder brother of one of the members of our prayer group, described some problems he was encountering in his life. I cannot remember the specifics; they seemed to be of a spiritual nature.

I asked John and a mutual friend to pray and fast. We planned a late afternoon visit to the home to deal with the situation. I later learned that the fasting may have been unnecessary. Matthew 17:19-20 states:

Then the disciples came to Jesus privately and said, "Why could we not drive it out?" And He said to them, "Because of the littleness of your faith; for truly I say to you, if you have faith the size of a mustard seed, you will say to this mountain, 'Move from here to there,' and it will move; and nothing will be impossible to you."

Verse 21 is parenthetical in the New American Standard Bible: "But this kind does not go out except by prayer and fasting." The notation states, "Early

49

manuscripts do not contain this verse."[16] In other words, fasting may have been a scribal addition to the original text. My friend, John, would have appreciated that statement. He later told me he "almost died" after going nearly 24 hours without food!

The three of us went to see Rickey. He gave greater detail to us about his situation: he wasn't sure of his salvation, he was afraid of losing his wife in divorce, and his entire life seemed to be falling apart.

Looking back on my experience with Stephan, the real action began when *I* commanded the devil to leave him alone. The four of us prayed together briefly. I commanded Satan, in the name and through the blood of Jesus Christ, to leave Rickey alone. The air in the room had previously been still. Suddenly, a powerful breeze blew out of the open window. Rickey, my two

---

[16] NEW AMERICAN STANDARD BIBLE®, Copyright © 1960,1962,1963,1968,1971,1972,1973,1975,1977,1995 by The Lockman Foundation. Used by permission.

friends, and I were amazed! I asked Rickey how he was feeling. He replied, "I am fine now!"

As we spoke further, we discovered that Rickey had become a Christian prior to our visit. I have since come to the conclusion that Christians can be just as *demonized* as lost people. The results are basically the same: the individual is controlled by the devil rather than the Holy Spirit of God. And we know that Satan has one primary item on his agenda, according to John 10:10a: "The thief comes only to steal and kill and destroy."

I have always enjoyed a little levity every now and then. The next morning I took a book off of my shelf by Dan Peters entitled, *Why Knock Rock? Is it bad? Is it Good? Does it Really Matter?* The book included several graphic representations; I selected an artist's rendition of a demonic countenance. I made several photocopies, pasted them on the back of my business cards, and placed a red circle with a diagonal line through it (a "prohibitory" sign) over the picture.

I handed the business cards to several people. One of

"Demon Busters"

them, a man named Gary, was a real jokester. He proclaimed, "You must be the Demon Busters!"

The copy machine subsequently broke down. We took it in for repairs; it worked for a few days and stopped again. Gary, ever the jokester, offered this advice: "Maybe you should run a picture of Jesus through the copy machine to get the demons out!"

We eventually realized the copy machine was beyond repair, and purchased a new one. Brother Jackie *highly* recommended that I refrain from copying similar pictures in the future.

The Surge

After three years in Alabama, the Lord led me to serve as pastor of a mission church in Toledo, Ohio. Twenty years earlier the church had been a thriving fellowship, but the membership had dwindled down to one older woman and one couple. The *really* bad news was that they were mad at each other.

I made a commitment to continue witnessing and to build a great church for the glory of God. Like Dr. Gray Allison, I soon developed my own story to keep me motivated to share the Gospel in Toledo. The man that lived in the house adjacent to the church was only 39 years old when he had a massive heart attack. I went to the hospital to visit him, and asked if I might tell him about Jesus Christ. He thanked me and said, "I would like to hear about Him. Let's wait until I get home and you can come over and tell me about it." I agreed to his request.

53

A few days later I was on top of the church building wiring in some security lights. Whenever anything was done around the church I was usually the one to do it! I saw the neighbor walking up his driveway followed by a man carrying a Christmas tree. The Lord said, "Go speak to him."

I thought, "I am wiring in these lights right now. I think I will wait until tomorrow." The neighbor, unfortunately for him and for me, died that night. And, as far as I know, he died without Christ.

My motto became, "Deadline with destiny." I believed that it was my personal responsibility to reach the more than 400,000 lost people in the city and to turn the church around into a thriving fellowship.

I should have read the travel brochure! The various reports I heard after my arrival in Toledo included: it was the "Witchcraft Capitol of the United States," it was one of three cities forming a "witchcraft triangle" in the United States, and the presiding witch over Toledo, Ohio, was a woman named Circé.

I could neither confirm nor deny the degree of Satanic activity in Toledo—all I knew was that my adventure in warfare was about to move up to a higher level!

The first place on my spiritual radar screen in the new pastorate was the church building itself. The atmosphere of the building could only be described as "dark." The pastor's office had recently been defiled by the sexual activities of a young man and his girlfriend; another room, adjacent to the baptistry in the front of the auditorium, also seemed to radiate with the presence of evil.

The only remedy I could imagine was to pray and claim the building for Jesus. I would walk around the church complex prior to each service, asking the Lord to wash the building above, below, and around with the blood of Jesus Christ.

The Sponsoring Pastor

I was disappointed by several problems I encountered upon my arrival in Toledo. First, I discovered that the church had been formed as a split from another church. I hate church splits! I also learned that I only had three remaining members, and they were mad at each other. I further discovered that the church had reverted to a mission status, and was now a "chapel" rather than a church. Finally, I noticed several unusual characteristics of the pastor of our sponsoring church. Later events clarified his real problem: he was, according to an impression I received from the Lord, a "lieutenant in Satan's army!"

The Chicago Trip

Shortly after I arrived in Ohio, I joined a group of several pastors in attending a conference several miles away in Chicago, Illinois. While we were away, my youngest daughter fell out of her bed and broke her clavicle, also known as her collar bone. My wife was agitated; she *really* needed me to be home with her. The details of the trip are found in my book, *Mercy: Surviving Ministerial Termination:*

> *As a young pastor, I attended a conference in a neighboring city with several other pastors from my local denominational association of churches. The group of pastors was large enough to require two full-size vans to transport them.*

> *[Craig Stokely], the elected leader of the local denominational association, was driving the lead van on our return trip home. I rode in the second van.*

> *["The lieutenant"] began to mock Brother Henry. "Look at the way he's driving. He's all over the road."*
> *The pastor in the passenger seat, "riding shot gun," agreed. "Yeah, he's getting too old" (the poor man was only 60 years old at the time).*

["The lieutenant"] expanded upon the theme of [Henry's] age. "It's time for him to retire. He's not an effective leader anymore. He needs to get out of the way so a younger man can take over." And [the lieutenant's] unspoken words were, "a younger man like me." And on and on it went for the three hours of our return trip.

At the next local denominational meeting, I raised my hand to make a verbal contribution. When I was recognized, I asked [Henry] to step out of the room. The poor man, living in a constant state of fear from having been attacked by pastors for several years, later said to me, "I thought you were going to call for my resignation!"

I looked at my fellow pastors scattered across the room and said, "I have heard a lot of criticisms toward Brother [Henry]. He can't drive; he's too old to do his job; he needs to retire."

"You may not respect the person, but you should respect his position. Maybe if you stopped criticizing him and started praying for him he would do a better job."

Brother [Henry] was brought back into the room and affirmed by the pastors. Amazingly, he did do a better job. And, just as amazingly, he retired a few years later with the honor he deserved. A pastor that leaves a church with honor is blessed; the church is also blessed by God for recognizing his contributions rather than his imperfections. [17]

The Business Meeting

Our first major victory occurred when a group from our sponsoring church arrived for a business meeting. As was my custom I had already prayed and bound Satan from our building. "The lieutenant," a man

---

[17] Matthew 10:41.

known to be highly articulate, conducted the meeting. His favorite word was "absolutely," which he pronounced "aaaab-sooo-lute-ly!" He was *absolutely* excited to come to the church—until he began to sense the power of God in the building! And then he was *absolutely* terrified.

The silver-tongued man began to stutter; he stumbled over his words; I think he may have broken into a sweat! Needless to say, he was miserable. My first impression was that he was not feeling well. His real problem was the fact he had crossed the "blood line," the area I had claimed for Jesus Christ. And because of the promise in 1 John 4:4b, "greater is He who is in you than he who is in the world," he was defeated the moment he walked through the door!

This trembling man approached me at the end of the service and said, "Scott, have you ever conducted a business meeting before?" I replied that I had. He said, "Well you can do them from now on—we won't be back!"

The Staff Meeting

A few weeks later I made a trip to the sponsoring church for a staff meeting with the pastor. "The lieutenant" asked me if his church could do anything to help us at our church. That would become an interesting question in light of the fact that, in more than four years of ministry, his church would never send one person or one dollar to assist us in the work!

I later discovered that one of his members had offered to place an advertisement for our church in the local newspaper. He told the lady that their church was already doing enough for us, and that she would simply be wasting her money! And this was supposed to be a *sponsoring* church?

I replied, "No, I think we have everything we need." The man immediately stopped talking; he entered a trance-like state; he tipped his head back and his eyes were glazed; he stared off into the distance. This was, to say the least, strange behavior!

He slowly swiveled his office chair around to face a table behind him. He reached out his hand and picked up a set of keys. He turned back to face me. He dropped the keys into my hand as he spoke in a mechanical, uninflected voice, "I g u e s s w e w o n ' t b e n e e d i n g t h e s e a n y m o r e ."

He offered no explanation as to the significance of the keys. I later discovered they were the only remaining set of keys his church had to our building.

The Diabolical Technique

Paul warns us in 2 Corinthians 2:10-11:

> *But one whom you forgive anything, I forgive also; for indeed what I have forgiven, if I have forgiven anything, I did it for your sakes in the presence of Christ, so that no advantage would be taken of us by Satan, for we are not ignorant of his schemes.*

"The lieutenant" certainly had his *schemes*; there was method to his madness. In fact, his approach was similar to the old Miller Lite™ beer commercial. As I recall, a man was walking through the stands at a ball game and spied a fan drinking the aforementioned beer. He sat next to the fan, pointed at his beer, and said, "This beer tastes great, doesn't it?" The fan said, "Yes." The man pointed a few rows away at another fan drinking the same beer. He said, "That's not what *he* says." The fan replied, "Oh yeah, what does *he* say?" The troublemaker said, "He says it's less filling." The fan rose from his seat, approached the other fan, and a fight began. The troublemaker smiled, rose from his seat, approached another victim, and the identical process ensued.

Whenever a new pastor would arrive on the scene, "the lieutenant" would meet and befriend him. When he thought that the pastor trusted him, he would ask about one of the new pastor's deacons: "How are you and Brother Williams getting along?" The new pastor would usually reply, "Just fine. Why do you ask?"

"The lieutenant" would then tell him some story about a problem between the previous pastor and Brother Williams: "He gave Brother Johnson, your predecessor, fits!" The new pastor would begin to trust "the lieutenant" and say something like, "Well, working with Brother Williams has been a little difficult." "The lieutenant" would ask, "In what way?" And the new pastor would load his wagon: he would tell him all about the area of conflict.

"The lieutenant's" next step would be—you guessed it—to approach Brother Williams. He would ask, "Do you know what your new pastor thinks about you?" And then he would load Brother Williams' wagon.

On more than one occasion, the squabble between the new pastor and the deacon would result in the disbanding of the church. "The lieutenant" would rise in an associational meeting and offer his condolences to "the fine people" of XYZ Church. He would then offer to help sell their building so that "the work of the Lord might go on." I thought, "How horrible!

This man is shutting down other churches so that he can pick up a few members for his own church!"

As I was praying years later, the Lord informed me that "the lieutenant" didn't care anything about increasing his own church's membership. His real motivation was that he had a real estate license; he was making a percentage every time he sold a church building.

I couldn't believe it! No one could *possibly* be that diabolical. So I sought confirmation. I approached the Director of Missions. I told him that the Lord had informed me that "the lieutenant" was destroying other churches in order to make a real estate commission from the various transactions. Brother Henry replied, "I have been watching the man for more than 18 years; that is exactly what he has been doing!"

Like Judas Iscariot, "the lieutenant" had sold his soul for thirty pieces of silver.[18]

The Grim Reaper

Three other pastors had spent time on various trips with "the lieutenant." One of them, his "minion"[19] had resigned as a pastor and was simply doing "the lieutenant's" bidding.

Another pastor, the leader of the Hispanic church in Toledo, Ohio, also spent some time with "the lieutenant" on a mission trip. He was later forced to resign his church. The Hispanic pastor told me, "I led every one of the people in that church to Jesus Christ. And then they fired me!"

The third pastor was a close personal friend of mine. This friend had once shared an unusual account of

---

[18] Matthew 26:15.
[19] The pastor riding shotgun in the section entitled, "The Chicago Trip," page 57.

personal spiritual warfare with me. He was addressing a group of teenagers in his church on a Saturday night; he gave a Gospel invitation; a young man responded. My friend spoke with him further about the next steps of a public decision, baptism, and church membership.

When my friend finished speaking, the young man asked him, "What should I do with my Satanic Bible?" My friend laughed. The young man said, "No, I'm serious!" And then he reached into his pants' pocket and produced a copy of the Satanic Bible. He asked again, "What should we do with it, pastor?" My friend replied, "I think we should burn it!"[20] "Okay pastor," the young man said.

My friend then told me, "Scott, we tried to burn it, but it wouldn't burn. I soaked it in gasoline, threw a lit match on it, and nothing happened!" The young man asked, "What do we do now, pastor?" My friend replied, "I guess we should pray." And they did.

---

[20] Acts 19:19.

My friend said, "As long as we prayed, the Satanic Bible burned; whenever we stopped praying, it stopped burning. So we continued praying until it was totally consumed!"

Two years later I sponsored a citywide prayer seminar. The speaker, Peter Lord, asked for the privilege of conducting a special meeting limited exclusively to pastors and church staff members. I made the arrangements.

The day of the pastors' meeting arrived, and my friend was in attendance. Peter shared a message of deliverance from the sin of lust. He told the story of how God had set him free from its bondage. He concluded with a story about a large meeting he had previously conducted with a group of pastors. He told them, "There is a man in this group today that is also struggling with the sin of lust. I am going to pray. When I finish, I want the man with the lust problem to look up at me." He told our group that, when he concluded, he looked into 500 sets of eyes.

He then said to us, "There is a man in this group today that needs to be set free. I am going to place a chair here in the front of the room. If that man is you, I want you to come up here and take a seat. The rest of us will pray and bind Satan's control from your life." A *different* friend of mine took the seat.

The meeting was concluded; my friend approached me. He said, "I should have been the man in that chair." I asked, "Why weren't you?" As he pointed to "the lieutenant" he replied, "Because *he* was here."

He continued, "About a year ago "the lieutenant"[21] and I went on an international mission trip together. During the course of the week I told him, 'Please pray for me; I am dealing with a serious weakness in the area of lust.' Scott, I never told anyone else! When I arrived home, my wife asked me, 'What is this I hear about you having a problem with lust?' So, even though I needed to be the one sitting in that chair today, I couldn't because *he* was here."

---

[21] My designation, not his.

Several months later my friend succumbed to his lust problem. He had an affair with a woman in the church; he lost his ministry as pastor of the church.

The Denominational Conference

One day the Director of Missions[22] contacted me. He said, "I am supposed to go to Atlanta for a conference, but I cannot attend. Would you go in my place?"

"Who else is going," I asked. He explained that "the lieutenant"[23] would also be going. I told the Director I would pray about it.

I really did not want to go. The three pastors that had spent considerable time with "the lieutenant" were all out of the ministry. I didn't want to be the next one! I prayed. The Lord asked, "If you don't go, whom do you suggest that I send in your place?"

---

[22] The designation for the leader of the association of churches in the Toledo area.

[23] My designation, not his.

I called the DOM and told him that I would go. "The lieutenant" and I flew to Atlanta and took a taxi to the hotel. As soon as we checked in, he walked into the bathroom and changed into his swimsuit! He said, "I will see you later!" And, although he was a married man, he literally ran to the pool to meet some women! He didn't return until long after I had gone to sleep.

I thought, "Oh, no! I have my prayer notebook in my briefcase—and his name is listed at the top of my 'lost and backslidden' section! What should I do?" And then I remembered my experience with him at the business meeting. I simply prayed that the blood of Jesus Christ would cover my briefcase. And then I went to sleep.

The next morning I awakened to discover my briefcase had been knocked over, and was halfway across the room. Apparently, "the lieutenant" had attempted to open it, and God wouldn't let him. I removed my prayer notebook and went to the lobby to pray.

71

The rest of our time together was rather uneventful. I had the opportunity to preach in a local church the next Sunday morning, and attend meetings the rest of the week.

The Reinforcements Are Coming, or Not!

A year later, one of the deacons from the sponsoring church telephoned me. He said, "Pastor, my family and I want to come and help you grow your church." I was ecstatic. I said, "That's great! We would be glad to have all of you!" He continued, "I would like to tell you my reason for coming." "Okay," I responded.

The deacon said, "I discovered that our pastor[24] is committing adultery with one of the women in the church. I confronted him with it, and he didn't deny it. Instead he said, 'There is nothing wrong with adultery!' I said, 'How can you say there is nothing

---

[24] A.k.a., "Satan's lieutenant."

wrong with adultery? Are you kidding me?' He said, 'No, the Bible says in Proverbs 6 that there are seven things that are an abomination to God; adultery isn't one of them.'" So the deacon said to me, "That's why we are coming to help you with your church." I repeated, "We would be glad to have you."

The deacon telephoned me again two days later. He said, "Pastor, I'm sorry—but my family and I won't be able to come to your church." I responded, "That's okay. You do what the Lord is telling you to do." He said, "I feel like I owe you an explanation." I replied, "No, you don't."

He continued, "I am going to tell you anyway. Last night, after I put the kids to bed, I turned off the light switch in my bedroom and walked toward the bed. Something grabbed me by the throat, threw me on the floor, and was choking the life out of me. I tried to pull it off, but to no avail. I finally cried out to Jesus, and whatever it was let go. I immediately ran to the light switch and turned it on; whatever it was that had

73

tried to kill me had gone." "Pastor," he said, "nothing could have *physically* gotten out of that room in the time it took me to turn on the light."

Finishing the story, he said, "Pastor, if my family wasn't involved I would come. But I can't expose them to *this*!" I told him that I understood.

Other Battles

"Licorice"   My piano player at my new church invited me to her home for a meal when I first arrived in Ohio. I went to the address I was given. I looked into a thicket and discovered the house was carefully hidden in its midst. The setup was reminiscent of the Addams' Family© house. I later discovered that the woman was involved in witchcraft!

We were all sitting around the dinner table when I heard a dog begin to howl in the basement. I asked,

"What's that?" The wife said, "That is our dog, Licorice." I asked, "Why is he in the basement?" She replied, "Because he doesn't know how to act around new people."

I forgot about the dog for a couple of years until, one night, I made a visit to the home. The husband opened the door without thinking. I looked into the doorway and there he was: the largest black dog I had ever seen!

"Licorice" ran directly toward me and lunged at my face. He was airborne when I reflexively raised my Bible to protect myself. He saw the Bible, diverted ninety degrees in mid-air—a physical impossibility—and ran off into the woods.

The Unlikely Convert

One of our faithful church members, Constance, had an unmarried daughter named Tori. Tori lived with a man named Justin; they were expecting a baby.

One particular Sunday, the Lord led me to read, without comment, from the book of Revelation. I was to start in chapter one, verse one, and continue reading until the time for the morning service had expired.

Justin and Tori came to church that morning for the first time. I began to read. I was in the middle of the third chapter when Justin jumped to his feet and ran out of the building. I later asked Constance, "What was wrong with Justin?" She answered, "He was wondering how you knew." I asked, "IIow I knew what?" She replied, "How you knew that the only book of the Bible he ever reads from is the book of Revelation?" I explained to Constance that I didn't know and that I was simply following God's leadership to read from the book that day.

Months later, on a Friday night, I was at the church building praying that the Lord would save Justin. The Lord said, "Go and see him." I asked, "Do you want me to go right now?" He replied, "Yes." I tried to explain to the Lord that Justin liked the party scene, and that he would not be home on a Friday night. The Lord assured me that he would.

I got into my car and drove to Justin's house; I knocked on the door. To my surprise, Justin answered. He asked, "Pastor, what are you doing out on a snowy Friday night?" I said, "God told me to come." Justin was taken aback; he invited me into his house and said, "He did? What does He want for you to talk with me about?" I shared Christ with Justin and, in a few moments, he was on his knees and praying to accept Jesus Christ as his Lord and Savior. Justin soon became a regular attendee at our church services.

I later discovered that Justin had spent some time in prison. He was now self-employed in the drywall business. One morning he asked me, "Pastor, what are you doing tomorrow?" I replied, "I don't really have anything I need to do. What do you need?" He said, "I was wondering if you would help me carry some drywall upstairs into an apartment building where I am working?" I said, "I would be glad to."

The next morning Justin and I began to carry drywall up the stairs. He liked my company and said, "Pastor, I think we should go into business together." Reflecting upon his time in prison I said, "What should we call it: pros and cons?" He laughingly replied, "Pastor, that wasn't very nice!" I thought, "And neither is carrying these double sheets of drywall up these stairs!"

The Prayer Meeting

I had the privilege of meeting Pastor Harold Meaux of Toledo Covenant Church. Harold was a real prayer warrior! Several of us would meet together at his church every morning for a time of intercession. Harold would play praise and worship music[25] for several minutes through the church's sound system.

---

[25] No words.

We would pray individually around the auditorium for several minutes. He would turn off the music as our signal to move to a cluster of chairs on the platform. No one spoke a word to anyone else; we just prayed. Harold would begin; another would pray and then another until everyone had finished. After we finished praying, we would have a brief time of fellowship. It was great!

After prayer one morning, a member of Harold's staff asked me if I had ever been involved in spiritual warfare. I told him of my limited experience. He said, "We have a lady that we have been working with, but to no avail. Would you go and see her?"

I agreed. I asked an older couple that had been visiting our church to go with me. We drove to the address and knocked on the door. A middle-aged lady invited us in.

After introducing my two companions, I said, "My friend from Toledo Covenant tells me you are having some strange occurrences here in your home." She said, "Yes I am! The first item is the strange noise I hear from time to time." I asked, "What kinds of noises?" "Creaking sounds," she replied. That was a real "ho-hum!" The house was at least 100 years old! I thought, "Creaking noises—she must be kidding!"

I asked, "Anything else?" She said, "Yes," there is one spot in my front yard where grass will not grow. The lawn experts have come out; they have planted seed, fertilized the area, and watered it. Nothing seems to work!"

That was another "ho-hum." I asked, "Anything else?" She replied, "Yes—there is one more thing." As she pointed, she asked me, "Do you see those dolls lined up against the wall over there?" I acknowledged that I did. "Do you see that each doll's head is a darker color than its body?" "Yes," I said. She continued, "My mother was a practicing witch. She poured some kind of syrup on their heads. They are not mechanical dolls, but several people have seen their heads turn."

I thought to myself, "Bingo! Now we have something!" I gave the usual disclaimer: "What I am about to do you might think I'm crazy—but you will have to get in line!" And then I began to pray. I bound Satan in the name and through the blood of Jesus Christ.

And then something unusual happened. The woman became terrified! Her eyes opened widely as she began to speak in an unknown tongue and make guttural, choking noises. She actually placed her hands on her own throat in an attempt to self-asphyxiate. I responded, "Oh, the problem isn't with the *house*—it's with the lady of the house!"

I had seen so much pain and suffering as a result of Satan's attacks on God's people that I thought, "It is my turn; it's payback time!" I said, "Come on demon: sing it with me. 'What can wash away my sin?

81

Nothing but the *blood of Jesus*!'" The woman began to make her choking noises again. I was having fun. I continued, "Now let's sing 'Power in the Blood.'"

Next, I picked up her telephone. I said, "I am calling a pastor friend of mine I used to know in Alabama. Perhaps you have heard of him? His name is Lee Clark."[26] She nearly shrieked! She became even more wild-eyed. I picked up the phone and dialed the number. I heard a recorded message: "I'm sorry, but that number is temporarily out of order." Thinking I had dialed the wrong number I tried again. I received the same message.

The lady that came with me had been praying in the kitchen while her husband was sitting in the room with the homeowner and me. She walked in and said, "The Lord has revealed to me that this lady has already been delivered."

---

[26] Not to be confused with Lee Castro.

I asked, "Then why is she still manifesting?" She replied, "Sometimes it takes a few days for the manifestations to end—but she has already been delivered."

Sadly, I believed what the lady told me. We left the house with the poor homeowner in the same condition as when we arrived!

I called my friend, Lee Clark, later that afternoon. The telephone rang three times. Lee answered, "Hello?" I said, "I am glad you finally have your phone line repaired." He asked, "What are you talking about? My phone has been ringing nonstop all day!" Satan truly is "the prince of the power of the air."[27]

Later that day, the Lord and I had a little discussion. Or, rather, He had a little discussion and I did a lot of listening. He asked, "Why are you so mad at the devil?" I replied, "Because of all of the lives he

---

[27] Ephesians 2:2.

destroys." The Lord's response: "Don't get mad at him; he is only doing his job." I thought, "What a curious statement." But as you, my dear reader, will soon see, that statement makes a lot of sense![28]

> **Lesson Number One**: Don't get mad at Satan; he is only doing his job.

The New Members

Many people have said that Satan is an active member of every church. I am not sure if that statement is correct, but I definitely remember the day that he joined the church in Ohio.

My wife and I both had full-time jobs, so we enrolled our youngest daughter, Susanna, in a daycare

---

[28] See the subsection "Alabama" under the heading "Final Frontier."

program. Susanna liked all of her teachers, especially "Miss Karen."

One day "Miss Karen" informed us that she would no longer be working at the daycare. We never really knew why. Several weeks later, on a Wednesday night, "Miss Karen" and her stepfather, Stanley visited our church.

I have always grimaced whenever a first time visitor arrived on the night of a scheduled business meeting; this night was one of those nights. We voted on several insignificant matters and then I said, "Tonight we need to elect a church treasurer. My wife, Diane, has been handling the church finances for several months and has asked to be replaced. Do we have any nominations?"

Stanley and "Miss Karen" were seated in the back of the room. Stanley raised his hand; I recognized him: "Yes, Stanley? We are glad to have you and Karen visiting with us. Do you have a question?" He said,

"No pastor, I just wanted to let you know that my daughter Karen and I are going to join the church tonight. And, for the record, I am an accountant."

I had apparently forgotten the old adage, "If it sounds too good to be true, it probably is." Instead I thought, "This is exciting! God is sending us an accountant to serve as our church treasurer."

I had learned a few tricks since I had arrived in Ohio. For one, I was a master moderator in a business meeting. I had observed the expertise of other pastors in local associational meetings as they handled items of business. One poor soul made the ultimate mistake. A committee chairman introduced a proposal. The moderator said, "We have a motion on the floor. The unenlightened man cried, 'Second.'" All eyes turned upon the man as the moderator said, "Committees bring their own second; no second is needed." I immediately purchased a copy of *Robert's Rules of Order*, and treated it as my "second Bible." As far as the implications for my church, for months I, as moderator, had made various motions. One lady pointed out that the moderator is not allowed to make a motion. I agreed with her and said, "I would like to *entertain* a motion that we do such and such." Someone else would then respond, "So moved"; that person would be on record as having made the motion.

This seemed like a good time to use my tactic. "I would like to entertain a motion that we elect Stanley to become our church treasurer." Someone said, "So moved," we voted, and Stanley was elected to the office. He and "Miss Karen" joined the church at the end of the service that night.

Just as the sponsoring pastor, "the lieutenant," felt uncomfortable in our church, Stanley also began to feel uncomfortable as well. In fact, Stanley became extremely depressed to the point of being physically ill.

I paid a visit to my sick church member. His wife, Gloria, was extremely concerned about Stanley. She attributed his sickness to the fact that he had been unable to work. She said, "Stanley is, by trade, an over-the-road truck driver. His dispatcher hasn't called him to drive in several weeks."[29] She asked, "Could you talk with him?" I said, "Of course." She led me to Stanley's bedroom; he was stretched out across the bed with his face turned away from the doorway.

I said, "Hello Stanley. What's wrong?" He replied without turning to look at me, "I'm just discouraged, pastor. I feel guilty that I can't work and support my family." I assured him I understood his feelings. He confessed that he was not really an accountant and had limited bookkeeping skills.

I said, "Stanley, we have been missing you and Karen at church. Do you think you will be back any time

---

[29] Note: Stanley would soon be selling his truck in order to open a lawn care business.

soon?" He looked at me and said, "I don't know if I will *ever* come back." I responded, "I hope you do, Stanley. But until you do, I will need to take the checkbook and let Diane[30] take over the books." Stanley rose out of bed and escorted me to the trunk of his car. He removed the checkbook, apologized again, and went back into the house.

Stanley returned to church several weeks later. Like "Ace,"[31] he looked better than any of us had ever seen him.[32] My wife gladly returned the checkbook to him. She told me that he was good at balancing the statements each month and, as a full-time schoolteacher, she certainly didn't need the added responsibility. Besides, she and I both were uncomfortable with the potential appearance of impropriety associated with her handling the church's finances.

---

[30] Diane: my poor wife.
[31] See the section entitled, "Failure," pages 44 and following.
[32] Matthew 12:43-45.

Months passed; I watched Stanley suspiciously. I kept praying, "Lord, what is going on in Stanley's life?" God never told me. And then, one Sunday morning, I preached a powerful message about repentance. Stanley was extremely nervous as he gripped the back of the pew in front of him. He did not respond during the invitation. I spoke with several of the members and then followed him to his car. In my typical jocular fashion I said, "Stanley, did you like that message this morning? The message tonight will be even better!" Stanley glared at me as he and his wife drove out of the parking lot. This would become Stanley's final warning to repent before God would reveal his hidden sin to me.

The next night my wife and I paid a visit to the home of one of Stanley's stepdaughters. Patricia gladly invited us into our home. I thanked her for her recent visits to our church; I asked her to come back in the future. Diane and I rose to leave; Patricia said, "Pastor, I think you and your wife had better sit down."

Diane and I returned to our seats. Patricia said, "Pastor, we have just discovered that my brother, Stanley, Jr., has been sexually abusing my little girl: his niece. We think it has been going on for three years, since she was only nine years old."

I said, "Patricia, I am so sorry!" And then I said, "I would like to ask you a personal question; you don't have to answer if you don't want to." She said, "What is it, pastor?" I asked, "Did Stanley do that to you?" She said, "Yes, pastor."

Just as John the Baptist leapt in Elizabeth's womb when Mary arrived with the news of Jesus' birth,[33] God's Spirit confirmed to my human spirit that what Diane and I were about to hear would be the truth. She continued, "On one occasion, Stanley invited his brothers to spend the night. He assigned each of us girls to be the 'wives' of these brothers during their visit. The brother I was assigned to took me upstairs and raped me. I came down the stairs, bleeding and

---

[33] Luke 1:41.

crying. I ran to my mother,[34] pointed at the trail of blood, and said, 'Mama, he hurt me.' She looked down with disgust at the blood on the carpet and said, 'You clean that up right now!'"

As I was praying the next morning, I realized that my next step in the process would be to confront Stanley with the news. I called him on the telephone and asked him to come to the church. He asked, "What is this about, pastor?" I replied, "I will tell you when you get here."

I hung up the phone and began to pray. I stepped outside of the church building and began to walk and pray. I was claiming the property for Jesus Christ, binding Satan, and releasing God's Spirit to do His work in the matter.

I have seen many cartoons that invariably show a man with a little devil on one shoulder and a little angel on

---

[34] Gloria.

the other. The devil tempts the man to disobey God; the angel encourages him to do what he already knows to be right. As I was walking, the devil began to speak; he said, "You had better think twice about this. Stanley sends his lawn care company to cut your grass for free every week." I glanced at the lawn; it *did* look good. Satan continued, "Who is going to do that if you confront him? *You* will have to do it!" Jesus said to "agree quickly with your adversary,"[35] and so I did. I thought, "Okay, I guess *I* will have to cut it."

Through the years I have discovered that fighting Satan is similar to playing a game of chess: move and countermove. He moved again: "And you have worked so hard to build this church. You will lose this church and it will close down. Don't do it!"[36] I wasn't ready for that one! I nearly stumbled as I thought of losing four years of hard work in rebuilding the church from three members to nearly 100 people.

---

[35] Matthew 5:25.
[36] Discover more about this principle in the section entitled, "The Chess Match."

And then the Lord said, "Think of Patricia's precious daughter and think of your own two daughters; are you willing to sacrifice the lives of innocent children to build *your* church? Forget about the church! By keeping this news a secret you will be exposing all of these children to Stanley's influence and the influence of his son."

And then I remembered a story my oldest daughter had told me. Stanley's son was playing in the church nursery with my youngest daughter. He said, "Let's pretend we are getting married. You can be my wife."

I nearly screamed as I thought about Stanley's brother "marrying" Patricia for the weekend. My resolve was restored; nothing Satan could say from that point on could possibly change my mind. I figuratively knocked the devil off my shoulder as I said, "No, Lord, I am not willing to sacrifice their lives!"

Stanley arrived a few minutes later. We walked into my office and closed the door. I said, "Stanley, let me tell you why I have asked you to come. I have been praying about you since you joined the church a year ago." He said, "Thanks, pastor."

I continued, "No Stanley, it's not good. I have been watching you. I have known that there is a serious sin in your life but, until now, I didn't know what it is." He apprehensively replied, "What is it, pastor?"

I said, "Stanley, you are a child molester!" He physically recoiled as he asked, "I am a *what*?" I continued, "You heard me, Stanley. You are a child molester." He demanded, "Who told you that?!" I answered, "God did."

A devilish grin formed on his face. He said, "God didn't tell you *anything*. Who told you?" I repeated, "God did." He said, "It's a lie. I am not a child molester!"

I continued, "Since you are denying the charge we will proceed to the next step." He asked, "What is that, pastor?" I said, "According to Matthew 18, I will need to bring another person to meet with you and me to discuss the matter; if you still refuse to repent, we will bring it before the church."[37] Stanley looked at me defiantly. He said, "Bring it on, pastor!"

And I *did*. Stanley left and I called one of the church leaders named "Craig." I told him the full story; he agreed to join me in a second meeting with Stanley. I telephoned Stanley and set the time for the meeting. I envisioned the three of us sitting down to settle the issue; I was wrong.

Craig arrived early so we could strategize. A few minutes later the door opened. Stanley walked in, but he was not alone! He had invited his wife, another stepdaughter, and a family friend and her daughter: five against two. Stanley introduced the family friend and her daughter. He said, "As you can see, I brought along a few witnesses of my own."

---

[37] Matthew 15:15-18.

I asked Stanley and his entourage to be seated. As they were sitting down, Stanley removed a cassette recorder from his pocket. He said, "My lawyer advised me to bring this." Not to be outdone, Craig replied, as he removed a smaller recorder from *his* pocket, "I also thought it would be a good idea." I thought, "I am glad I brought Craig with me to this meeting!"

I began, "Stanley, the reason we are here is to discuss the fact that you are a child molester." The stepdaughter looked pleadingly at me and said, "Pastor, why are you trying to destroy our family?" I answered, "I am not trying to destroy your family. I am trying to uncover the truth."

And then Stanley repeated his earlier question, "I am going to ask you again: who told you that I am a child molester?" I again replied, "God did."

The discussion lasted for nearly thirty minutes. Finally, the family friend raised her hand. "Yes,

Dianne," I said. She looked at Stanley with disgust as she spoke: "Stanley, I have heard all of this that I want to hear. I am not going to let you threaten this pastor anymore. We all know that everything he is accusing you of is true! You *are* a child molester! You go ahead and take this pastor to court; I will testify on *his* behalf!" And then Stanley's family friend apologized to me.

The cassette recorders were turned off. Stanley and his group left the building. Craig and I looked at each other in amazement. We prayed and thanked the Lord. Satan, for the moment, had been defeated.[38]

The next item on my agenda was to minister to Patricia and her daughter. The little twelve-year-old girl would be required to testify against her uncle in court. I prayed fervently for her; this would be extremely difficult for such a young girl.

---

[38] Luke 4:13.

In the meantime, I was also praying for Stanley. As I was praying, I remembered the following passage from the Bible that addressed Paul's dealings with a similar incident of *extreme* immorality:

> *In the name of our Lord Jesus, when you are assembled, and I with you in spirit, with the power of our Lord Jesus, I have decided to deliver such a one to Satan for the destruction of his flesh, so that his spirit may be saved in the day of the Lord Jesus.*[39]

I said, "Lord, I am doing that for Stanley!" He responded, "That's fine, but you have to tell him." I shouted, "You want me to *tell* him? Why?" The Lord said, "You can't deliver someone to Satan without letting them know what you are doing, and giving them an opportunity to repent."

Obediently, I left the church building and climbed into my car. I drove to Stanley's house and knocked on

---

[39] 1 Corinthians 5:4-5.

the door.   Stanley's son-in-law, the husband of the stepdaughter that had accompanied Stanley to the meeting, answered the door.   He looked at me and said without hiding his disgust, "What do *you* want?" I replied, "I want to speak to Stanley."

Stanley called out, "Who is it?"   The son-in-law responded contemptuously, "*Pastor's* here."   Stanley said, "Let him in."

I walked past the son-in-law; Stanley was already seated at the kitchen table.   He asked, "What do you want to talk about?"   I laid my Bible on the table with the text facing him.   I recited the verse from memory: "I have decided to deliver such a one to Satan for the destruction of his flesh, so that his spirit may be saved in the day of the lord Jesus."   I reached over, closed my Bible, picked it up, and said, "Stanley, I am doing that for you."   I rose from the chair, turned my back to Stanley and his astonished family members, walked out of the house, and closed the door.

Stanley's son was subsequently arrested and charged

with sexual abuse. Stanley and his family literally bankrupted themselves by selling all of their lawn care equipment in order to pay for his son's defense.

The trial began. We were told that, because of her age, Patricia's daughter would be allowed to give her testimony on videotape so that she would not have to see her offender in court. Stanley's defense attorney challenged the recording by stating that his client deserved the right to face his accuser in court. The mediator relented.

We all waited outside the courtroom as a brave twelve-year-old girl marched, alone, into the room. She told the mediator what he needed to hear. Her testimony, coupled with unshakable documentation provided by the medical examiner, produced a guilty verdict. Stanley's son was going to prison! Satan was certainly "destroying Stanley's flesh," as he lost both his livelihood *and* the trial of his only son.

The second part of the verse was apparently fulfilled a year later. I received a request for Stanley's church letter; he wanted to transfer his membership to another church in the area. Many pastors would have been thrilled to remove someone like Stanley from their church roll; I could not, in good conscience, shift my problems to someone else.

I called the pastor of the other church. I said, "I understand that Stanley and his family have joined your church." He said, "Yes, that's right." I asked, "Do you know why they left *our* church?" He replied, "Yes, he told me." I continued, "Did he tell you that he is a child molester?" The pastor said, "Yes, he told me everything. He has been attending our church this past week during revival services, has repented, and now desires to live for God." I said, "That's great, and I hope it is true. But I don' care how much he *says* he wants to live for God, don't you *ever* let him around children again."

The pastor agreed to my terms; I instructed our clerk to send the letter. I thought, "Maybe Satan *has* destroyed his flesh and the Lord *has* saved his soul. Wouldn't that be great?" The main thing is to keep the main thing the main thing.

Restoration

One of my favorite Bible verses is Joel 2:25, "Then I will make up to you for the years that the swarming locust has eaten, the creeping locust, the stripping locust and the gnawing locust, my great army which I sent among you." I believe that God is in the business of restoring His churches, his people, and their ministries.

Transforming the Atmosphere

I formerly subscribed to a monthly preaching series on cassette tape known as "Quest Tape of the Month™."

One of the first sermons I received was by Jack Hayford, pastor of the Church on the Way in Van Nuys, California. Providentially, the message concerned changing the atmosphere in a church building!

Jack told a story from one of his former pastorates. A member of the church had given him the initial guided tour of the facilities. And then the man said something rather unusual to Jack: "Brother Jack, I am a veteran of two wars. I don't fear anyone or anything. But when I turn the light switch off over there and walk to the door over here, something scares me to death!" Jack said in the taped message, "I knew exactly what frightened him, but I didn't tell him. There was an obvious demonic presence in that building!"

Jack continued, "I knew the secret to changing the atmosphere of the building. Every day I would go into the auditorium and sing praises to my Lord, Jesus

Christ. I was all alone, except for my unseen audience. I knew the Lord was there, but others were present as well."

Jack explained that, over time, the spiritual environment began to change. The building itself seemed to be transformed from a place of darkness into a place of light. People began to notice the difference as the presence of the Lord filled the auditorium, and lives were changed for the glory of God.

I took that message to heart! I began to play Christian music in our church building throughout the week. I would sing along with the lyrics. I particularly remember singing "We Shall Behold Him," by Sandi Patti. I wept as I thought about the soon coming of the Lord Jesus Christ!

And, just as Jack described, little by little the spiritual darkness began to lift and the spiritual light began to shine. One of our members, a man named Bob, had a background in Rosicrucianism—a form of spirit worship. As a believer in Christ, he still seemed to have an increased awareness of spiritual matters. He looked at me one morning through eyes filled with tears and said, "He's here, isn't He, pastor?" He was, of course, referring to the presence of God. I replied with tears filling my own eyes, "Yes, Bob, He's here!"

His Churches

As I mentioned, the church in Ohio that God led me to was a split from another church. I was extremely disappointed. As I have also mentioned, I hate church splits. They are a very loud testimony against God's transformational work in the lives of people.

As I prayed about the situation, the Lord directed me to a passage in the book of Daniel. Daniel was not personally guilty of the sins for which he was confessing. But, as a member of the nation of Israel, he included himself in their sins. Seventy years after the sins of the Israelites had resulted in their Babylonian captivity, he prayed in Daniel 9:4-6:

> *Alas, O Lord, the great and awesome God, who keeps His covenant and lovingkindness for those who love Him and keep His commandments, we have sinned, committed iniquity, acted wickedly and rebelled, even turning aside from Your commandments and ordinances. Moreover, we have not listened to Your servants the prophets, who spoke in Your name to our kings, our princes, our fathers and all the people of the land.*

The next Sunday morning, I publicly confessed my vicarious involvement in the church split to the members of my congregation. I asked their permission to meet with the pastor of the original church for the purpose of confessing our guilt to him, and they agreed.

I approached the pastor of the other church, a man named Brother Bob; I apologized to him for all of the hurt and suffering our church had caused to the members of his church. He was astonished; he said, "You weren't here when all of that happened, and neither was I." I responded, "I know, but the testimonies of both of our churches have been hurt by the division. May I have permission to speak to your church members to give them a public apology?" He allowed me to address his congregation; the pain and anger that had been associated with the two churches immediately vanished.

I later discovered that some of the same people that left Brother Bob's church had also left my church in anger. Once again, I approached the pastor of the church where they had "landed." I again asked for permission to speak to his church members so that I could apologize for the wounds they had received at my church. Once again, the second pastor allowed it; once again, the animosity between the two churches mysteriously disappeared.

His People and Their Ministries

My friend[40] had an affair and lost his ministry. His wife and two children, however, chose to remain with him. He became angry and bitter. He resigned his church; he and his family members were allowed to temporarily remain in the pastor's home. As a result of his misplaced anger, he began to physically abuse his wife.

I paid him a visit. I said, "I understand you have been hitting your wife. The next time you feel like hitting somebody, give me a call. I will come over and you can hit me. But I warn you: I will hit you back!"

God was not through with my friend. He sought Christian counseling through a chapter of Pure Life Ministries™ sponsored through a local church of another denomination. After a year he told me that he believed he was ready to reenter the pastorate.

---

[40] See the section entitled, "Grim Reaper," on pages 67 and following.

I gave him the following advice: "I think you and your family should move your church membership from your previous church to my church." He asked, "Why should I do that?" I replied, "Because representatives from your *previous* church will tell the search committee members from your *prospective* church about your indiscretion. I, on the other hand, will tell them that you have been a faithful member of our church. Which of the two responses would you prefer that the committee members would hear?"

He understood my reasoning; he and his family joined our church. Several months later, my friend was called to serve as pastor of another church. Restoration![41]

[41] Joel 2:25.

Bonnie McMinn

Our church hosted several short-term missions' groups throughout the years. On one occasion, we had a group of teenagers come from Prince Avenue Baptist Church in Athens, Georgia. They spent hours praying in the auditorium each day; they surveyed and witnessed to the residents in the community.

Youth from Prince Avenue

Toward the end of the week I told their leader, Doug Nix, "The church is yours. I want you and your youth group to decorate it any way that you like." He smiled and said, "Really? You want us to take over and transform this place?" I said, "Yes."

I Have Come to Give You a Future and a Hope
Jer. 29:11

The Banner

The young people from Prince Avenue were motivated! They took down the individual globes from the chandeliers and washed them by hand; they vacuumed the carpets; they polished the furniture; they even scrubbed the toilets. And then they left their mark: they placed a banner at the back of the church with the words, "'For I know the plans that I have for you,' declares the Lord, 'plans for welfare and not for calamity to give you a future and a hope.'"[42] The group left; months passed; we all forgot about the banner.

A year later the Lord brought a wonderful lady named Bonnie McMinn to serve in the Toledo area. Bonnie was to become the director of the Maumee Valley

---

[42] Jeremiah 29:11.

Outreach Center, an inner city ministry of the association of Baptist churches in Toledo, Ohio. She did a tremendous job with the Outreach Center. She had one rule for receiving assistance: a person was required to hear a sermon before they received a box of food. She and her assistants would interview people, asking the number of people each of them had in their families. If they said, "four," the workers would fill enough boxes to feed a family of four.

Bonnie and her workers would then say, "Have a seat here in this room. A pastor will give you a message from God's Word. When he is finished, we will call your name and give you your box of food."

Most of the people would stay, but some would leave during the sermon. Bonnie would call the names of the people to receive their food. If no one replied she would say, loudly enough to the workers so that all could hear, "Okay, go place the contents of *their* box back into our inventory for someone else to receive." The word spread quickly: "Don't go to the Maumee

113

Valley Outreach Center if you don't want to hear a sermon."

All of the local pastors prayed that she and her daughter, Aaron, would join their particular church. They knew she would be a worker. Many pastors, in fact, had openly pursued Bonnie and Aaron by taking them out for a meal and inviting them to visit their churches.

One Sunday morning she and Aaron arrived at our church. I was actually surprised to see them. At the end of the service I gave the invitation, and they joined our church. I later asked, "I know you and Aaron could have joined one of the larger churches, and they would have been excited to have you. Why did you join our little mission church?" She replied, "It was the sign in the back of the auditorium." I was puzzled; I asked, "What sign?" She said, "You know: the banner with the Bible verse on it—Jeremiah 29:11."

Our family was truly blessed by Bonnie and Aaron. Aaron instantly became friends with my two daughters. Bonnie and my wife, Diane, also became friends; they both joined the local exercise club, and took water aerobics classes together. Diane later told me, "Bonnie was exactly what I had been praying for. I had said to the Lord, 'Please send someone to the church that sincerely loves Jesus.'" And He did!

Bonnie was not only an answer to Diane's prayers, but also to mine. She observed the "one man show" for a few weeks: I drove the church van, taught the adult Sunday school class, led the worship, preached, taught the evening Bible class, made all of the church-related visits, and whatever else needed to be done. She finally said, "Pastor, you are killing yourself. Would you allow me to lead the music?" I said, "Sure Bonnie!" And she did. Several weeks later she said, "You are still doing too much. May I teach the Sunday school class?" Again I said, "Yes."

Lee Castro

I had the privilege of serving as the preaching evangelist in a friend's church in Arkansas. That is when I met *him*: Lee Castro.[43] Lee is a very interesting man. He is an American born of Hispanic parents; he is also bilingual. He is extremely gifted in singing, and was the worship evangelist selected to work with me during a revival I conducted in Arkansas.

Lee Castro

The host pastor printed some revival flyers to distribute to the people of the community. He, several church members, Lee, and I left the church and walked through the little town; we talked to people as we went. The host pastor entered a local café; Lee

---

[43] Not to be confused with Lee Clark, referred to in the section entitled, "The Prayer Meeting."

and I were right behind him. Lee began to play a song on his guitar and to sing a song about Jesus. The host pastor and I were aghast! Lee then said, "We are here to invite you to the revival service tonight at First Baptist Church. These men[44] will give you a flyer with the details." The pastor and I nervously complied.

We left the café. The rest of the church members joined us as we walked down the street to an outdoor auto repair shop. Lee walked up to a mechanic wearing a shirt with the name "Bill" clearly embossed on the pocket. Lee said, "Hello, Bill. Is that your name, Bill?" Bill pointed to the monogram. He said, "Yes, it's printed right here on my shirt. It says, 'Bill.' And that is my name: 'Bill.'"

I thought, "This is going to be interesting. The man is already becoming angry."

---

[44] Referring to the pastor and me.

Lee continued, "Well, it's nice to meet you, Bill. We are from First Baptist Church. We would like to invite you to the revival services starting tonight." Bill replied, "I appreciate the invitation, but I won't be coming." Lee said, "Why not Bill? Tell me why not."

Bill's countenance visibly changed as he said, "Since you have asked me I will tell you. My mother used to beat me and make me go to church. My 16th birthday was on a Sunday. I said then, 'I will never go back to church.' I have never gone back, and I never will!"

Lee continued, "That's where you are wrong, Bill. One day you are going to die. They are going to place you in a casket and roll you down the aisle of a church. But it will be too late for you to hear the Gospel and be saved; you will be burning in Hell!"

Lee gave Bill a moment for his words to sink in and then he said, "Regarding what you said about your mother beating you, and making you go to church: my daddy used to beat me and make me go to school. Guess what, Bill? I have a college degree. My mother used to beat me and make me brush my teeth. Guess what, Bill?" Lee took his finger, swiped it across his lips, and said, "I still have all of my teeth!" And then he moved in for the kill. He said, "My daddy used to beat me and make me go to church. And then, one day, I fell in love with Jesus. Now I want to go to church!"

Bill said, "I expect you and everyone else with you had better leave right now!" Lee replied, "Before I go, Bill, could I sing a song for you about Jesus?" Bill said, "I don't want to hear your song. In fact, I don't want to hear another word out of your mouth." Lee, as if he had not heard Bill's warning, began to strum the guitar and sing. I moved slowly away; I knew the fight was about to start. But, to my surprise, it didn't.

As we walked away, I said to Lee, "Weren't you afraid he was going to hit you?" He replied, "No, he *couldn't* hit me." I continued, "Do you really believe he couldn't hit you?" Lee said, "One time a man was so angry with me that he had his fist raised above his head to hit me. I rebuked him in Jesus' name. The angels held his arm so tightly that he couldn't move. So I obviously wasn't worried about what Bill might try to do to me."

A year later I scheduled a series of revival services at the church in Toledo, Ohio. I asked Jackie Shelton[45] to preach, and Lee Castro to lead the worship. Brother Jackie stayed in a local motel; Lee stayed in our home.

Lee and I were reminiscing about the revival in Arkansas when he remembered a joke. The joke, I am sad to report, was of a questionable nature.[46] I said, "Listen, Lee, you might be able to get away with telling jokes like that where you come from in Texas.

[45] The pastor I served with in Moulton, Alabama.
[46] Pastors have a tendency to tell improper jokes to other pastors.

But you are in Ohio now, and the demons here are really powerful!" He immediately became serious as he said, "I rebuke that in Jesus' name." I asked, "Rebuke what?" He continued, "I rebuke your statement. My Jesus is more powerful than every demon here in Ohio or anywhere else. As a child of Jesus Christ, I refuse to accept Satan's authority over my life." I was confused, but I apologized. I would soon discover that Lee *did* have authority over the forces of darkness. In fact, he would teach me a valuable technique that I would effectively use on several occasions on the foreign mission field.

Lee made two suggestions for the week of revival. He asked, "How many people do you believe God will save this week?" I said, "After much prayer, I think we will have fifty people give their lives to Jesus." Lee said, "Then why don't you challenge your people to give $100.00 per family; that will amount to only $2.00 per soul."

I thought, "Our members only gave a total of $25,000.00 last year. They will never give $100.00 per family in one week!" I said, "I don't think they will give that much." Lee said, "Probably not, but they won't give $5.00 either. They will give $20.00 or more." I agreed. At the end of the week the people had given a total of $2,300! Needless to say, *I* was amazed.

Lee also suggested, "Let's schedule some time with some of the members of your church for lunch during the week of revival. That way we can talk about the revival and generate some interest."

I made appointments to visit in the homes of several families, including the home of an older man I recently had the privilege of leading to faith in Jesus Christ. As we were driving to the house, I told Lee, "This man's aunt might be there—and she is *really* strange!" "Strange in what way," he asked. I replied, "She always accuses me of believing in three gods. She denies the Trinity, and thinks people should be baptized in the name of Jesus only." Lee said, "If she is there I will be ready for her." She was there, and he was ready!

We walked into the house, and there she sat. She looked at Lee, pointed at me, and said, "I guess you believe like *he* does." He answered, "How is that ma'am?" She replied, "You know: that there are three Gods."

He said, "Ma'am, I used to believe like you do. But then I realized that the blood of Jesus does *this*, and the blood of Jesus does *that*." As we talked with the older man and his wife for another thirty minutes, the aunt never said another word.

We ate lunch and left their home. Lee asked me, "Did you see what I did?" I replied, "Yes, but I thought you had to *shout* in order to bind Satan." Lee continued, "No. *You* knew what I was doing, *I* knew what I was doing, and *the devil* knew what I was doing—but the other three had no idea."

Lesson number two: Satan can be bound by

conversationally mentioning the blood of Jesus.

> **Lesson Number Two**: Satan can be bound by conversationally mentioning the blood of Jesus.

More exciting than the aunt's response, however, were the responses of the revival attendees to the Gospel. Lee and I had been praying that God would save 50 people that week, a tall order for a church that never had more than 100 in attendance. At the conclusion of the final service, 42 people had prayed to receive Jesus Christ as their personal Lord and Savior! Added to our previous decisions, Diane and I had witnessed the conversion of more than 200 precious souls in our four-year ministry together in Ohio.

The Chess Match

I learned to play chess as a teenage boy. My next door neighbor, Pat Whitworth, would defeat me on a regular basis. And then, one day, I decided to trick him. I read an article, entitled "Chess," in our old 1960s version of *The World Book Encyclopedia©*. I read that the Russian chess master, Boris Spassky, had defeated one of his opponents in only six moves. I memorized the moves and made quick work of Pat! He asked, "How did you do that?" I lied to him; I said, "I guess I was just lucky." Pat said, "No, you weren't just lucky. How did you do it?" I told him about Spassky. I don't think he ever played chess with me again.

I played chess intermittently throughout the years. I taught my son, Mike, how to play. It didn't take him long to learn; he was soon able to beat his own father. Once I began to be involved in spiritual warfare, I discovered that Satan was also an avid chess player.[47]

The time came for our church to constitute: to break our ties with "the lieutenant's" sponsoring church. We took a delegation consisting of several of our church members that included my wife, Bonnie McMinn, and me. We presented our case; the leaders of the sponsoring church denied our request.

I determined that our next course of action should be to reject their verdict and constitute our church without their permission. I approached the new Director of Missions, a man that "did not know Joseph."[48] He was friendly toward "the lieutenant," and somewhat withdrawn from me. I have two reasons that have since confirmed my suspicions:

1. "The lieutenant's" church was larger than ours and gave more money through the local association.

---

[47] See the section entitled, "The New Members," on pages 86 and following.

[48] Exodus 1:8.

2. Years later my wife overheard a conversation between an Ohio pastor and this former Director of Missions. The pastor asked, "I heard great things about Scott's church. Why did they close the doors?" The DOM replied, "Because of the attitude of the people."

I asked the Director, "If we constitute our church without the sponsoring church's blessing, will we be allowed to join the association?" He basically replied that it would be a crapshoot: "something (as a business venture) that has an unpredictable outcome."[49] He said, "You would have to present your request to the credentials' committee; they would have to decide whether or not to make a recommendation to honor your request." He continued, "And the odds would probably not be in

---

[49] MERRIAM-WEBSTER'S COLLEGIATE DICTIONARY AND THESAURUS, DELUXE AUDIO EDITION®, Version 2.5, Copyright © Merriam-Webster, Incorporated, 47 Federal Street, P.O. Box 281, Springfield, MA 01102.

your favor."

At that point I didn't care. I was totally unconcerned that we might not be recognized by the association as a church, or that we might have legally lost our building to the "mother" church. It was time to make the move.

And then Bonnie McMinn told me, "Pastor, I am with you in whatever decision you make. If you choose to constitute without the sponsoring church's permission, Aaron and I will go with you." The devil and his throng began to cackle in Hell. He must have said, "I have him now. If he chooses to constitute the church, Bonnie will follow him. And he knows that the association will relieve her of her duties at the Outreach Center." Satan must have been smiling as he whispered to me, "It's your move."

I agonized in prayer over my decision for days. I was faced with only two possible alternatives: I could allow our church to remain in its ungodly connection to the sponsoring church, or I could risk Bonnie's outreach ministry and constitute without permission. Satan thought, "Either way, I have him!" And then I remembered a story:[50]

> *Two men in a museum noticed the painting of a chess game between a man and the devil. The man had only one piece left. The title of the artwork was Checkmate. One of the patrons, a chess champion, was bothered about the painting. After studying the art for a lengthy period, it dawned on him. The king had one more move.*

I, like the man in the story, had one more move. And Satan would never anticipate this one. He never does. Satan is selfish; he never sacrifices himself for anything or anyone. He didn't understand Jesus' sacrifice on the cross, he didn't understand Stephen's

---

[50] John Ortberg, *When the Game Is Over, It All Goes Back in the Box,* (Zondervan Publishing, 2009), pg. 6.

response at his stoning,[51] and he doesn't understand today when a Christian unselfishly gives himself and surrenders his dreams for the benefit of another. But I finally saw my one additional move. I could sacrifice four years of ministry as pastor, and resign. After much prayer, I resigned.

Within a year after my resignation, Satan's prophecy was fulfilled. The church closed its doors and, to my knowledge, more than twenty years later has never reopened in that capacity.

The good news is that Bonnie remained as the director of the Maumee Valley Outreach Center for another decade. Many people trusted Jesus Christ through her faithful ministry there, and she left it in very capable hands. She has since served as a missionary to Africa.

Always remember: when playing chess with Satan, you always have one more move: self-sacrifice.

---

[51] Acts 7:60.

Lesson Number Three: When playing chess with Satan, you always have one more move: self-sacrifice

Phase Three: Confrontational Evangelism

My family and I returned to Alabama in 1992. I served, once again, as one of two associate pastors of the same large church I had ministered in after graduating from the seminary. I did not sense a great spiritual battle. The warfare tools became a little rusty and so, sadly, did the tools for evangelism.

I encountered a new adversary: the flesh. In another book entitled, *Mercy! Surviving Ministerial Termination*, I wrote:

> *I remember the story about Charles Haddon Spurgeon sitting in the balcony of the institution that bore his name: "Spurgeon's College." A young man was preaching a message about the spiritual armor in Ephesians chapter six.*

132

The other students were amazed at the visual picture the young man was painting! "You could almost hear the pieces of the armor 'clank' as he put them on."

"And then," the student cried, "he draws his sword. And now, where is the enemy?" Spurgeon leaned over the rail and said, "He's in the armor!"

The greatest battlefield I have ever encountered has been the enemy within! I am my own greatest opponent! I became unmotivated. I saw few people coming to Christ as a result of my personal witness. I finally quit trying to win people to Christ, and surrendered in defeat to a life of spiritual malaise.

Seven years later I reentered the pastorate. I made several contacts, sent résumés, and spoke with representatives from several churches. After much prayer, I felt led to one particular church. The members of the pastor search committee asked me to preach four messages, two morning services and two evening services, so that everyone would have an opportunity to hear me. They also asked me to prepare for a "town hall," question and answer session.

The four messages were well received. I prepared for the "town hall" by asking the Lord, "What is my vision for this church?" He said, "To learn to love Jesus and take as many people with you on the journey as want to go."

I remember fielding several questions. One lady finally asked, "What is your vision for our church." I replied, "To learn to love Jesus and take as many people with me on the journey as want to go." The woman began to weep. I was thrilled at her response; the devil, as we would eventually see, was not.

All of my messages and all of my efforts for our first year together were focused upon learning to love

Jesus; they were well-received by the members of the congregation. As I prayed about next steps, the Lord led me to follow this progression—learning to love:

❖ Jesus.
❖ Each other: appreciating the other members of the church.
❖ Our community: winning the lost to Christ.
❖ Our world: member involvement in missions.

The Start

I immediately knew in my spirit exactly when the opposition would begin. Satan is not threatened when God's people love Jesus; neither is he particularly threatened when they learn to love one another. But his kingdom is definitely endangered when God's people reach out to the community with the Gospel of Jesus Christ.

So I enjoyed my first two years as I dealt with the themes of loving Jesus and loving other Christians within the church. But the third year finally arrived. I began to preach about God's calling upon every one of our lives to share our faith with the unsaved. We instituted the F.A.I.T.H. strategy for evangelism.[52] We began with three trained team captains;[53] slowly but surely additional members received the training.

We had limited success during the first two semesters of F.A.I.T.H. Everything changed radically, however, as we began our third semester. We began to see several adults come to faith in Jesus Christ. And not just *any* adults—alcoholics were being saved; a church member actually approached me in the fear that, if he didn't get saved immediately, he would die and go to Hell! In a church with an average attendance of 150, more than twenty people gave their lives to Christ and were baptized during that year.[54]

---

[52] http://www.lifeway.com/n/Product-Family/FAITH-Evangelism.

[53] Four underwent the training process, but one moved to another city before we implemented the program.

[54] Without having the customary revival services.

Not surprisingly, leading the church became more difficult; I could sense the resistance coming from many of the church members. I employed the old methods of spiritual warfare that I had cultivated in Ohio: I walked around the perimeter of the church building, asking the Lord to cleanse the building with the blood of Jesus; I regularly walked through the empty auditorium, praying for the people by name that would fill the pews during the church service. Much to my dismay, things just seemed to worsen.

I asked the Lord why the "old tricks" weren't working. He replied, "The problem isn't the devil; these people are just mean!" God apparently wasn't kidding. Unknown to me, members of the two senior adult Sunday school classes were polled by their teachers with the question, "How many of you think it is time for our pastor to leave." The teachers started by asking my known opponents, and then moved around their rooms to ask the undecided members of their classes.

The next step occurred in the monthly deacons' meeting. Eight of us were in the room, including seven deacons and me. One of the deacons proposed that I be asked to resign; three others immediately concurred. The remaining three deacons were astonished. They had no idea that the motion would be introduced in the midst of their routine discussions; they, however, were clearly outnumbered. One by one, the three men resigned from their positions as deacons and left the room.

After much prayer, and consultation with several godly men, I later chose to resign. During the last few weeks leading up to my resignation, however, Satan joined in the fray! My daughter, Kelly, reported that her stove turned on by itself when she wasn't home; my wife told me that the radio was regularly turning itself on and off. I laughingly thought, "Satan, what a puny attempt to frighten my family!"

I have discovered that there is very little difference between an attack from Satan and an attack from a fleshly Christian. And that is not to say that the devil is not involved.[55] In fact, a few weeks later I exposed his role in the situation. I told the church members in a morning service that two or three people had been motivated by Satan to recommend my resignation; those people, in turn, had motivated others.

During the service my wife and two daughters said they heard people murmuring in the room in the guttural voices typically associated with demonic control. Satan was definitely in the house!

I announced my resignation later that day at the end of the Sunday evening service.

The Surge

My next pastorate was a time of *personal* restoration. The Lord led me to work with a church filled with

---

[55] Apparently, the prayers of the saints in the "Bible Belt," the southern portion of the United States, have forced Satan to resort to utilizing more covert tactics.

people that genuinely loved and respected my family and me; they nurtured us back to spiritual and emotional health.

During my three-year tenure at that church, and with the encouragement of Dr. Steve Wilkes, I became personally involved in foreign missions. Wilkes, as he likes to be called, is a professor of missiology at Mid-America Baptist Theological Seminary, and founder of Word-wide Church Planters.[56]

Brazil

The church members voted to pay for my first foreign mission trip in 2003; I went to Brazil. When our team arrived, we split into small groups with translators and went into the village of Teresina to share the Gospel. Hundreds of people prayed the sinner's prayer. I was hooked!

---

[56] An organization specializing in planting churches around the globe, www.wwcp.org.

I was soon to discover that, like Toledo, Ohio, the foreign mission field is rife with demonic activity. A couple of nights after we had arrived, we held a revival service in a storefront church. Another team member was preaching when a drunken man noisily staggered up. I placed my arm on his shoulder and motioned for him to sit next to me. He constantly attempted to disrupt the meeting by pointing and staring at various women in the crowd. I simply placed my finger over my mouth as I said, "Shhh!"

After the meeting, I asked one of our female translators[57] to help me talk to the man. I asked him through her if he could say, "Jesus Christ is Lord." The translator said, "He keeps on saying, 'Jesus Christ is *your* Lord.'"

"Catherine Zeta"

---

[57] Wilkes jokingly described her as "looking like Catherine Zeta-Jones with bad teeth."

I asked him several times to say the words; he continued with the same refrain. And then the translator became horrified! I asked, "What's wrong?" She said, "He can understand what you are saying!" I replied, "Yes—so what?" She whispered, "He doesn't speak English!" I explained, "No, but *Satan* does; he is fluent in several languages!"

She said, "I can't do this anymore!" And then she ran and fell, trembling and crying, into the arms of our group leader.

Lesson number four: Satan is multilingual. You can bind him in any country in any language by the mere mention of the blood of Jesus!

Lesson Number Four:
Satan is multilingual.

Several months later Wilkes contacted me again and asked me to make a return trip to Brazil. I agreed.

We landed in São Paulo and worked for a couple of days on the outskirts of the city. On the first night Wilkes invited all of us to his hotel room for a time of sharing. Two members of our team told of an encounter they had, that day, with a witch. They said, "She has a statue of 'Black Jesus' in her house;[58] she is known in the community for practicing voodoo and other magical rituals."

I was thrilled at the news! I approached Wilkes, our team leader; I said, "Could I go with that team tomorrow? I believe I can help set the witch free from Satan's control!" And then I reminded him of my previous experiences in spiritual warfare.

---

[58] An idol associated with occult practices.

Wilkes wisely replied, "I have no doubt that you could

L-R: Dimas, Eloy's son & wife, Eloy

set her free, but how long do you think it would take?" I said, "Maybe a couple of hours. Why?" He asked, "How many people could you lead to Christ in two hours?" I thought for a minute. I said, "Brazilians are so responsive to the Gospel: probably 25 to 30 people." He then asked, "What, do you think, would be the best use of your time— working with one woman, or seeing 25 people accept Jesus Christ as Lord and Savior?" Once again, the old saying came to mind, "The main thing is to keep the main thing the main thing." I conceded his point.

Lesson number five: don't let spiritual warfare distract you from the main thing of winning souls to Jesus Christ!

> **Lesson Number Five:** Don't let
> spiritual warfare distract you from the
> main thing of winning souls to Jesus
> Christ!

Wilkes asked for two volunteers to go to a little village named Elias Fausto. Another man, Velton, and I raised our hands.

We were transported to the village to work with a 32-year-old seminary trained mission pastor named Eloy Da Costa Fraga, Jr.; we stay in his home with his family.[59] Eloy told my visiting partner and me through our translator, Dimas, that he was glad that we had come; he then informed us, however, that our work would be greatly restricted.

I asked, "Can we witness to people on the streets?" "Yes," he replied, "but with one restriction: you cannot ask anyone to be saved."
I was, to say the least, a little angry. My visiting

---

[59] For the record: Eloy's wife was an excellent cook!

partner and I retired to our room after the meeting. I said, "I didn't pay $1,000.00 to come to Brazil and waste my time. If things don't get better soon, I am joining the rest of the group back down in São Paulo!"

The next morning we went to the local school and received a tour of the facilities. We were introduced to the principal and several of the teachers. I looked around and saw hundreds of boys and girls that desperately needed the Gospel! We were told that we would be sharing the Gospel with the children later in the afternoon. Again, the restriction from Eloy, the host pastor: "You can witness to them but you cannot ask them to be saved."

When we returned, I remembered a technique I had observed on my first trip to Brazil. Our team had been invited to meet with the mayor of the small town of Forteleza. John Goldwater, our group leader really schmoozed him! He said, "We are honored to meet with the mayor of this town! We know that you are a busy man, and that you have the great responsibility of leading all of these people." We all watched as the mayor began to smile. He was being honored by people from the United States! He and all of the members of his family ultimately accepted Jesus Christ as their Lord.

Prepared to use the same technique, I asked to see the principal. The secretary explained that she had been called away. As we were being escorted through the office complex, I spotted the principal. I asked, "Isn't that the principal?"

The secretary replied, "Yes, it is. She must have come back into her office without my knowledge." I asked, "Could we speak to her for a moment?" The secretary said, "Of course," as she led us into the principal's office. Addressing her supervisor, she said, "These men would like to see you."

The principal beckoned us into her office. I said, "We are honored to be in your school today. We are especially honored to meet with you! You have the responsibility of leading all of these children and all of these teachers. You are truly a great leader!"

She smiled broadly as I continued, "We would like your permission to talk to these boys and girls about our faith in Jesus Christ, and then invite those who are interested to pray and receive Him as their personal Lord and Savior." I didn't speak much Portuguese, but I understood her clearly as she excitedly said, "Sí!"

My visiting partner and I first shared about our faith in an assembly setting; we then moved from room to room, inviting people to accept Christ. Several boys and girls indicated that they had accepted the Lord; I asked them to write their names on a list so we could pray for them.[60]

---

[60] And so the mission pastor could do the follow-up.

We moved into the last room on our schedule. Velton had finished sharing the Gospel; the boys and girls were following him as he led them through the sinner's prayer. I heard an older lady praying near the doorway. I thought,

L-R: Velton, the principal, Scott

"Maybe one of the teachers is being saved."

We were leaving the room when I heard a voice behind us, saying in choppy English, "Me too; pray for me too!" I turned around to look. It was the principal!

I asked Dimas what she was trying to say. He explained that she had also been saved; she wanted us to add her name to the list and to pray for her, too!

Eloy was overwhelmed. I could see that he was eager to learn how to share his faith. After supper that night I told him, through our translator, "I am lost. Please tell me how to become a Christian." He was puzzled. I repeated my statement, "I am lost. Please tell me how to be saved." He smiled and then, using the techniques he had learned by observation from Velton and me, he proceeded to go through the process of leading me to faith in Christ.

The next day Eloy, Velton, Dimas, and I were sharing our faith door-to-door in the community. We alternated: Velton shared at one house; I shared at the next. Little by little we included Eloy in the process. Before the day was over, he was on fire! Imagine that? A soul-winning pastor.

Eloy left us in the afternoon to attend a meeting in São Paulo. Velton, Dimas, and I walked up to a house and found three men standing in the front yard. Velton attempted to witness to them; one of the men kept interrupting him. The man would say something in

Portuguese and show us an amulet he was wearing around his neck.

Dimas grew impatient. He said, "We are wasting our time. Let's go!" I stepped in; I said, "Not yet. Tell him that I like his amulet but that, because of the blood of Jesus, I personally couldn't wear one."

Dimas reluctantly did as he was instructed. The man folded his hands, lowered his head, and walked backward until he was leaning on the railing in the front of the house. He never said another word. We shared with the two remaining men, and they both accepted Jesus Christ. We left.

Velton looked at me and shouted, "What did you do?" With feigned innocence I asked, "What do you mean?" He demanded "You know exactly what I mean." I replied, "Oh, I guess you are referring to the way I conversationally mentioned the blood of Jesus Christ?" He said "Yes, I thought you had to shout in order to bind Satan in the name of Jesus!" I replied, "That's what I *used* to think." And then I divulged my experience with Lee Castro and the aunt with the "three gods" in Toledo. Lesson number two applied!

> **Lesson Number Two:** Satan can be bound by conversationally mentioning the blood of Jesus.

Velton and I were given a hero's sendoff by Pastor Eloy and the members of his congregation. I was personally given two gifts: a framed picture of their native tree, the ipê roxo, and a bookmark with the pastor's handwritten message on the back: "Deus enviou vou para abençoar Elias Fausto; Nossa gratidão por tudo que fizeste. Não nos esqueça, pois não esqueceremos vou. Pastor Eloy e Igrega Batista Elias Fausto S. P. Brazil, 08/03/05."

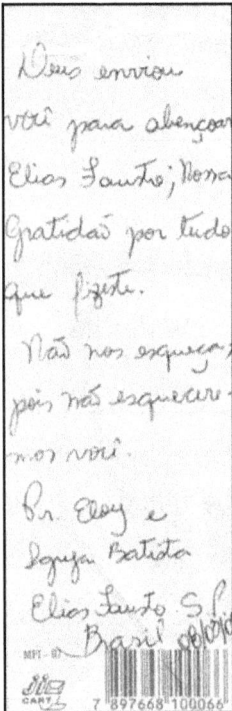

152

The rough English translation is, "God has sent I am going to bless Elias Fausto. Our gratitude for all that you have done. We do not forget that, because we shall not forget I will." Pastor Eloy and the Baptist Church of Elias Fausto, São Paulo, Brazil, August 3, 2005.[61]

After Velton and I returned to join the rest of the group in São Paulo we were informed that our results had been truly amazing. It seems that the people of Elias Fausto were heavily into witchcraft and Satan worship. We had spent very little time binding Satan as we effectively shared the Gospel. Lesson number five revisited.

> **Lesson Number Five:** Don't let spiritual warfare distract you from the main thing of winning souls to Jesus Christ!

---

[61] http://translation.babylon.com/english/to-portuguese, site visited on 10/6/2011.

What a blessing! At the end of the week our team in its entirety had recorded 524 decisions for Christ.

Ecuador

I was asked to lead a rather uneventful trip[62] to

Ecuadorian children with bracelets

Ecuador. Our team consisted of three of the members of my church, one of my daughters, and five people that joined us

from a church in Texas, and me. We used witnessing bracelets to share with large groups of people. We handed people one bead at a time, explaining the meaning of each color: the black bead illustrated sin, the red bead represented Jesus' cleansing blood, the

---

[62] At least from a spiritual warfare perspective.

white bead described their hearts after they accepted Jesus Christ, and so on.

The trip was *extremely* eventful from the perspective of evangelism. At the end of the week we had counted more than 1,000 decisions for Christ.

Peru

I had the additional privilege of leading a trip to Lima, Peru. Two church members and my oldest daughter, Kelly, accompanied me.

We spent the majority of our time "street witnessing." In one week our team of four missionaries recorded more than 300 decisions of people praying to receive Christ!

We ran into some spiritual opposition during the trip. Each of the team members encountered a different drunk on their first day of sharing. I explained that the devil invariably sends an alcoholic to interfere with our witness on foreign trips. I instructed them to simply mention "the blood of Christ," and to continue sharing Christ with the people.

They all returned with the same report: "A drunk staggered up in the middle of my presentation. I simply said the phrase 'the blood of Jesus,' and I continued to witness. When I finished, the man had mysteriously left the crowd and had disappeared!"

Frustration

My most recent pastoral experience was diametrically opposed to the healing time my family and I had experienced at the previous church. I remember telling my wife, as we were leaving the former church, "I will regret this one day." And the "one day" came much more quickly than I had anticipated!

I continued to be personally involved in short-term foreign mission trips. My first experience occurred when I was asked to lead a group to the Dominican

Republic. I have called this "the mission trip from Hell!" Whatever could have *possibly* gone wrong *did* go wrong.

Five female church members, my youngest daughter, Susanna, and I left the church in Alabama a little later than we had originally planned on our way to the Birmingham airport. We barely arrived at the airport in time to go through security and get on the plane.

We were standing in line at the airport when my wife telephoned me on my cell phone. I asked, "What's wrong?" She said, "Susanna's dog "Bo' has just been run over and killed by a car. I told Susanna. We offered to take her back home, but she was a trooper! She said, "No, I still want to go."

We boarded the plane, began to taxi down the runway, and then stopped for over an hour! The pilot came over the intercom and said, "We will be delayed on our takeoff because of the weather situation in Atlanta."

By the time we arrived in Atlanta we had already missed our connecting flight to Santo Domingo. What was the *really* bad news? The airline only offered one flight per day to the Dominican Republic. Oh well—we would only be one day behind schedule! And the airline paid for our food and lodging!

The next day we arrived in Santo Domingo. We met with the mission pastor and a missionary from the International Mission Board. The IMB missionary told my team to do exactly as the pastor instructed us. We gave the pastor's wife enough money for meals for the week.[63]

We drove about an hour north of town and checked into the "motel."[64] We checked out the next morning, paid the bill, and checked into the Howard Johnson's Motel in Santo Domingo.

---

[63] These meals, unfortunately, were poorly prepared. I later developed the worst case of "Montezuma's Revenge" ever recorded!

[64] Actually a cluster of one-room, one-bath brothels!

We wasted the entire next day stamping the host pastor's church name on the back of the Gospel tracts we brought with us. That night, I was invited to preach to a group of around 75 in the courtyard of the mission pastor's house. My topic, interestingly, was "the blood of Jesus Christ."

I looked for the pastor after the message, but he was nowhere to be found. I asked his wife if she had seen him. She said, "He is sick and had to go to bed."

On the way back to the Howard Johnson's Hotel, my daughter told me that the pastor had been behaving strangely during my sermon on the blood. "In what way," I asked. She said, "Do you remember the devil walking through the crowd during the scourging scene in the movie, 'The Passion'©?" I replied, "Yes." She continued, "The pastor looked *exactly* like that. He was standing behind you swaying back and forth and staring, through reddened eyes filled with hatred, at the back of your head!"

The next day we were asked to stamp the church name on tracts again. I told the translator I wanted to speak with the pastor; I then explained to the pastor that we had already stamped more than enough tracts for us to distribute; we had come solely for the purpose of witnessing to the people in his community. He acquiesced. We went to a nearby village, split off into small groups with translators, and shared with the locals.

The female translator that my small group was working with that day seemed to know everyone in the community. Whenever we attempted to approach a group of people she would say, "These people are already Christians." Becoming exasperated, I finally said, "Let these people tell us that." And we had the opportunity to lead a few people to Christ.

The translator's phone rang. She explained that one of our team members had become sick. We assembled together, climbed onto the bus, and drove until we found a mission clinic; the doctor on call gave our ailing team member two units of saline.

The next morning we put the team member on a plane back to Alabama. We drove back to the pastor's house and went out, once again, to witness. This time we had a *good* translator—or so I *thought*! He was fluent in English, and had an immediate rapport with the locals. There was only one problem: every time we asked the "obligating question,"[65] his telephone would ring. He would excuse himself for a minute; the prospects would lose interest and walk away.

After three interruptions I demanded, "Who keeps calling you?" He replied, "The pastor of my church down in Santo Domingo; I am an electrician and he needs some advice." I asked, "Does your pastor know that we are out sharing Christ? I think what we are doing is a lot more important than your pastor's electrical situation!"

---

[65] "Would you like to accept Jesus Christ as your Lord and Savior?"

We led a few people to Christ before our translator received another phone call. This time it was the mission pastor; he instructed our translator to bring us back to his house. "Why," I asked. The translator replied, "I think more of your team members have become sick."

We went back to the house. A couple of our team members *were* suffering heat exhaustion from the tropical climate, but they were still ready to witness. I asked, "What's going on?"

One of the team members said, "We led one lady to faith in Jesus Christ, and she was really excited. Then the pastor began to speak to her; he spoke for thirty minutes! When he finished. she looked really confused."

Each team basically told the same story: the mission pastor had "pulled the plug" on their attempts to witness. I walked up to the mission pastor and motioned for the translator to join us. I towered over the little pastor as I said to the translator, "Tell him this: unless the Lord changes my mind, we will be leaving tomorrow!"

Our team members met together that night to discuss the day's events. One of the ladies said, "I didn't want to say anything, but your translator has been acting inappropriately toward me." I dismissed him the next morning when he called me on the telephone. I said, "We won't need your services any longer."

We boarded the plane and returned home. This certainly had become the "mission trip from Hell!" And, as nearly as I could tell, Satan had won that round.

The Final Frontier

Uganda

In the midst of the trial I had the privilege of going with a group of pastors and laypeople to Uganda. The team consisted of fourteen people: a family of four, a husband and wife, two ladies, three men, and three pastors. Jaime Boyachek, our team leader, did a tremendous job in preparing us for our trip. We knew exactly what to expect, or did we?

The primary purpose of the mission trip was to carry on a three-night evangelistic crusade in a remote area filled with more than a thousand refugees. The refugees came and stood for hours as we pastors alternated preaching in the services. As a result, hundreds of people indicated they had received Jesus Christ as their Lord and Savior.

Satan was definitely present. Two men that attended the services each evening were extremely angry; in fact, they were more than angry. Several members of our team noticed the looks of hatred that filled the eyes of both men. One of the other pastors looked at me and said, "Wow! Look at that guy over there." I informed him that the man was, more than likely, demon possessed.

Each morning the pastors would alternate preaching to local pastors and their spouses, as well as the members of a few local churches. As I preached a message from the parable of the soils, I became aware that there might be problems back home.[66] I symbolically opened my hand to give everything I had to the Lord: my house, my family, and my finances. I then said, "My church," and I began to weep. I knew exactly what that meant: I would soon lose my church.

---

[66] Matthew 13:3-23. The message is entitled, "Preaching in Uganda," and may be found, in three parts, at http://www.walterscottmoore.com/video-sermons.html.

We were still in Uganda on the following Sunday. Nassan invited me to preach in his church. I was led to the passage in 1 Peter 5:6-9:

> *Therefore humble yourselves under the mighty hand of God, that He may exalt you at the proper time, casting all your anxiety on Him, because He cares for you. Be of sober spirit, be on the alert. Your adversary, the devil, prowls around like a roaring lion, seeking someone to devour. But resist him, firm in your faith, knowing that the same experiences of suffering are being accomplished by your brethren who are in the world.*

Years earlier, Bill Gothard observed that the *roaring* lion is "the elderly lion that has no teeth. The job of this old, toothless lion is to make a lot of noise; he scares the prey toward the young lions." Gothard further stated, "The young lions kill the prey, and share the spoils with him."

I explained that the safest place in spiritual warfare is

face to face with Satan; that, like the old lion, we should run *toward* him rather than *away* from him. I called one of the men from our team to help me illustrate the point. I began to make strange faces and roar into the microphone as I inched ever closer to my prey. At first, he moved away. And then, suddenly, he turned; he began to approach *me*. I roared more loudly and made more hideous faces, but he kept coming. He came all the way into my personal space; I whimpered, turned, and ran away. Nassan's congregation learned an important lesson: "Don't fear Satan; resist him and he will flee from you."[67]

After the service, our team members walked from the auditorium to the pastor's study. Along the way we saw a man, on a hill above the church, tied to a tree. I asked, "What's his story." One of the church leaders replied, "The man has lost his mind. His family members bring him here each morning and tie him to that tree."[68]

---

[67] James 4:7.
[68] Mark 5:2-15

I looked at one of the ladies in our group that had expressed interest in spiritual warfare. I asked her if she was ready to cast out her first demon. "Yes," she said excitedly. We went up to the top of the hill; the lady spoke to the man through a translator as I coached her through the process. She bound Satan in the name and through the blood of the Lord Jesus Christ. She then gave the man the ultimate test of genuine deliverance: she asked him to say, "Jesus Christ of Nazareth is Lord," to which he replied, "Jesus Christ of Nazareth is Lord." We were later informed that, on the very next Sunday, the man was seated, "in his right mind," in the church.

The Greatest Enemy You Will Face

I have discovered through this process that there is an enemy greater than Satan himself. Satan is limited in the width of his path of destruction; he must first receive God's permission before attacking one of

God's saints.[69] As a result, I believe he has devised a better plan: to stir up *people* and then release them to do his bidding. People "in the flesh" can be much meaner than the devil ever thought about being. As Adrian Rogers said on more than one occasion, "If Satan were to die tomorrow, we have enough meanness to keep us going until Jesus comes back." To which I heartily reply, "Amen!"

David illustrated his understanding of this truth in 1 Chronicles 21:13: "I am in great distress; please let me fall into the hand of the Lord, for His mercies are very great. But do not let me fall into the hand of man." In other words, "I will take my chances with an angry God over my chances with a group of angry people."

The most effective weapons we can use against Satan are the mere mention of the blood of Jesus and a willingness to die for Him.[70] But the only way the

---

[69] Job 1:6-12
[70] Revelation 12:11.

flesh can be defeated is through the power of the Holy Spirit of the living God. The secret is found in Galatians 5:16-17: "But I say, walk by the Spirit, and you will not carry out the desire of the flesh. For the flesh sets its desire against the Spirit, and the Spirit against the flesh; for these are in opposition to one another, so that you may not do the things that you please."

Satan has always used treacherous religious leaders to do his bidding.[71] And he will always use those leaders to stir up the crowd. The same fleshly people that will cry, "Hosanna"[72] when you arrive will eventually cry, "Crucify him" when you leave![73]

What is the proper response to their rejection? Jesus gave us the pattern in Luke 23:34a: "Father, forgive them; for they do not know what they are doing." He prayed for their salvation. The people were convicted

---

[71] John 8:31-45.
[72] John 12:13.
[73] John 19:15.

of their sin by the words of Peter's sermon in Acts 2:36-37:

> *"Therefore let all the house of Israel know for certain that God has made Him both Lord and Christ—this Jesus whom you crucified." Now when they heard this, they were pierced to the heart, and said to Peter and the rest of the apostles, "Brethren, what shall we do?"*

The people repented,[74] and Jesus' prayer for their salvation was answered. If you will follow His pattern of forgiveness, many more people in your generation will be saved as you pray for them today.

The Greatest Lesson I Have Learned

Months have passed, and I have had the opportunity to apply the famous "20-20 hindsight" principle to the

---

[74] Acts 2:38-41.

situation. am well aware of the admonition from Jesus' half-brother, the leader of the first century church at Jerusalem, found in James 1:19-20: "This you know, my beloved brethren. But everyone must be quick to hear, slow to speak and slow to anger; for the anger of man does not achieve the righteousness of God." I know that anger has effectively taken my focus off of Jesus and has directed it toward Satan and his servants. As a result, I have forgotten that "the main thing is to keep the main thing the main thing."

This morning, as I was penning these words, the Lord reminded me about lesson number one: don't get mad at Satan; he is only doing his job. And then He took it one step further; he said, "Don't get mad at Satan's *servants*; they, too, are only doing *their* jobs."

In order to understand *their* jobs, I asked the Lord, "What exactly *is* Satan's job?" His reply, "Satan is the bottom-feeder in the church." I immediately thought of a catfish cleaning the algae from the bottom and sides of an aquarium.

I remembered Proverbs 14:4: "Where no oxen are, the manger is clean, but much revenue comes by the strength of the ox." The verse means that problems in a church will increase proportionately to an increase in the number of people. I concluded, "God has assigned to Satan and his servants the job of cleaning up the mess left in the tank by all of the *fish* (church members)."

And then I checked the definition of bottom-feeder in the dictionary. A bottom-feeder is "an opportunist who seeks quick profit usually at the expense of others or from their misfortune."[75] Not only does that clarify Satan's motivation, it also defines the motivation of his servants: they *all* benefit from the pain God's people inflict upon each other in the church. So today, for the first time, I have learned *my* most important lesson: "don't get mad at Satan's

[75] MERRIAM-WEBSTER'S COLLEGIATE DICTIONARY AND THESAURUS, DELUXE AUDIO EDITION®, Version 2.5, Copyright © Merriam-Webster, Incorporated, 47 Federal Street, P.O. Box 28l, Springfield, MA 01102.

servants; they are only doing *their* jobs."

> Lesson number six: Don't get
> mad at Satan's *servants*; they are
> only doing *their* jobs.

So, my dear reader, walk daily with the Lord in prayer. Listen for His voice. Do what He says. Go out and win the unsaved to Jesus Christ. Resist the devil.[76] Expect opposition. But *always* have a greater expectation: that you and the kingdom of God will prevail, and souls will be saved!

---

[76] James 4:7.

TABLE ONE: The Six Lessons

1. Don't get mad at Satan; he is only doing his job.
2. Satan can be bound by conversationally mentioning the blood of Jesus.
3. When playing chess with Satan, you always have one more move: self-sacrifice
4. Satan is multilingual.
5. Don't let spiritual warfare distract you from the main thing of winning souls to Jesus Christ!
6. Don't get mad at Satan's *servants*; they are only doing *their* jobs.

Bibliography

1. http://translation.babylon.com/english/to-portuguese, site visited on 10/6/2011.
2. http://www.lifeway.com/n/Product-Family/FAITH-Evangelism.
3. http://www.rondunn.com/Biography.htm, website visited on 9/24/2011.
4. MERRIAM-WEBSTER'S COLLEGIATE DICTIONARY AND THESAURUS, DELUXE AUDIO EDITION®, Version 2.5, Copyright © Merriam-Webster, Incorporated, 47 Federal Street, P.O. Box 28l, Springfield, MA 01102.
5. *Mid-America Baptist Theological Seminary*, 2011 Catalog.
6. NEW AMERICAN STANDARD BIBLE®, Copyright © 1960,1962,1963,1968,1971,1972,1973,1975,1977,1995 by The Lockman Foundation. Used by permission.
7. Ortberg, John. *When the Game Is Over, It All Goes Back in the Box*, (Zondervan Publishing, 2009).

About the Author

W. Scott Moore

During a ministerial career of more than three decades, Christian author W. Scott Moore, Bachelor of Business Administration, Master of Divinity, Doctor of Ministry, has served as a bus minister, children's pastor, youth minister, associate pastor and senior pastor. He was, most recently, the senior pastor of a rural church in north Alabama.

www.ingramcontent.com/pod-product-compliance
Lightning Source LLC
Chambersburg PA
CBHW070957040426
42443CB00007B/553